THE NEWCOMERS SERIES

HISPANICS IN U.S. HISTORY

1865 TO THE PRESENT

VOLUME 2

GLOBE BOOK COMPANY
Englewood Cliffs, N.J.

USING SOCIAL STUDIES SKILLS

Front cover, clockwise: Joseph Montoya, Mercedes O. Cubría, Luis Muñoz Marín, Felisa Rincón de Gautier
Design: Function Thru Form Inc.
Photo research: Omni-Photo Communications, Inc.

Printed in the United States of America
10 9 8 7 6 5 4 3
ISBN 1–55675–587–2

Globe Book Company
A division of Simon & Schuster
Englewood Cliffs, New Jersey

C O N T E N T S

Chapter 1 AFTER THE CIVIL WAR

AIM: How were Mexican Americans affected by the migration of Anglo Americans to the Southwest after the Civil War? How were their lives changed?

Read the text to answer the AIM question(s).

1. In the years following the Civil War, many Anglo Americans settled in what are today New Mexico, Arizona, California, and Texas. They came to the Southwest to look for gold, build homes, and raise cattle on the open ranges. The **Mexican Americans** welcomed the new settlers. They taught them new ways to mine gold and silver. They showed the Anglo Americans how to brand cattle and tame wild horses. They also showed them how to irrigate the land.

2. Why, then, didn't the Anglo Americans live in peace with the Mexican Americans? Instead, they often treated them with suspicion. They looked on the Mexican Americans as foreigners who spoke a different language. They felt the Mexican Americans had strange customs that they did not understand.

3. Many Anglo Americans wanted the lands that had long been owned by the Mexican Americans. They took advantage of the fact that often the Mexican Americans did not understand American laws. Those laws were

The first sentence in each paragraph gives the main idea.

▲ This wedding photo was taken on a ranch in Texas about 90 years ago.

The caption will help you understand the illustration.

2

in English. Many Mexican Americans, according to the law, had not registered their property. Nor had they paid taxes on their land. Their land titles became worthless under American laws. The Anglos bought up their land. By the 1880s, Mexican Americans in California owned only one-fourth of the land that they had owned before 1848.

4. Along with their land, Mexican Americans also lost their political power. Before the Civil War, they held a number of political offices at all levels of government. Now most of these positions were taken by Anglos. In New Mexico, the Mexican Americans were still in the majority. To keep control of New Mexico, Anglos worked to keep it a territory. The United States government appointed Anglos to most political offices in New Mexico territory. Anglos delayed statehood until 1912.

5. The wealthy Mexican Americans, called *ricos,* kept their land. Some of them joined together with Anglo bankers and merchants to run the territory. Known as the "Santa Fe Ring," this group controlled every part of New Mexican life. They cheated and stole from the majority of Mexican Americans who lived in poverty.

6. In most towns and cities of the Southwest, two separate peoples lived. The Anglos lived in the better part of town with their own schools and stores. The Mexican Americans lived in the poor part of town. They called their sections *barrios,* the Spanish word for neighborhoods. The two groups lived separately.

7. In the late 1800s, a large number of Mexicans entered the American Southwest. Many Mexican Americans, especially the *ricos,* felt they were better than these new **immigrants.** To separate themselves from the newer immigrants, many Mexican Americans began to call themselves *Hispanos,* or Spanish Americans. In California, people from these older families called themselves *Californios* to separate themselves from the newer immigrants. Hispanos started to blend into Anglo-American culture.

Vocabulary words are defined in context ne and are al found in tl Glossary.

Study tip To review, reread the first sentence in each paragraph. Also review the time chart on the back cover.

Understanding What You Have Read

Check your comprehension by doing these activities.

Choose each correct answer and write the letter in the space provided.

_____ 1. *ricos*

_____ 2. *Hispanos*

_____ 3. *barrios*

_____ 4. The Santa Fe Ring

_____ 5. gold

_____ 6. land

a. Hispanic Americans who had lived in the Southwest for many years before the United States took it from Mexico

b. what many Anglos hoped to find in the Southwest

c. wealthy Mexican Americans

d. what some Anglos took away from Mexican Americans

e. rich group of Anglos and Mexican Americans who controlled New Mexico

f. poor Mexican–American neigborhoods

Each chapter has one of these activities: **Building Geography Skills, Linking Past to Present,** or **Daily Life.**

Linking Past to Present

▲ This is a Mexican-American homestead in New Mexico in the 1890s.

The Importance of Land. After the United States won the Mexican War, the **Treaty of Guadalupe Hidalgo** was signed in 1848. The treaty gave the United States the **Mexican Cession,** which was one-third of Mexico. This land included what are today the states of California, Nevada, and Utah, and parts of New Mexico, Colorado, Arizona, and Wyoming. Under this treaty, Mexican Americans living in those areas were to be made full citizens of the United States. They were also to be given property rights. However, during the late 19th century, many Mexican Americans lost their land to Anglos because they could not prove ownership. Often families ended up working the land for others or moving to the cities to find new jobs. Today, Mexican Americans are full citizens whose right to own property is recognized.

1. What states were included in the Mexican Cession? _____

_____

2. What happened to Mexican Americans who lost their land? _____

_____

Spotlight on People

Juan Nepomuceno Cortina. In the 1900s, a number of Mexican American bandit-revolutionaries fought to right the wrongs committed against Mexican Americans. One of the most noted bandits was Juan Nepomuceno Cortina. He was also known as "Ceno" or the "Red Robber of the Rio Grande" because of his red beard.

Surprisingly, Cortina began his life as one of Mexico's privileged citizens. He was a rancher and a wealthy landowner. He belonged to an upper-class family. After fighting on his country's side in the Mexican War, Cortina settled down on a ranch near Brownsville, Texas.

In 1859, an event took place that was to change his life forever. Cortina saw a fellow Mexican being beaten by a Texas marshal in Brownsville. When the marshal refused to stop, Cortina shot and wounded him. News of Cortina's bold act spread quickly. Soon he was a hero to poor Mexican Americans throughout the Southwest. But now Cortina himself was a hunted man. He was forced to flee across the border into Mexico to escape punishment.

A few months later, he returned with a band of Mexican volunteers and took Brownsville by force. He raised the Mexican flag and issued a "declaration of **grievances**" against Anglo Americans. Soon Cortina's band was being hunted by the Texas Rangers, the local militia, and the United States Army. The officer in command of the army was Robert E. Lee.

Cortina managed to escape from all his enemies. He returned to his native state of Tamaulipas in northeastern Mexico. There he served as acting governor for a time. The great Mexican president Benito Juárez made Cortina a general in the Mexican army.

But Cortina's days of glory were numbered. He was arrested for cattle rustling in 1873 and jailed without trial in Mexico City. He spent most of his remaining years under local arrest.

Called a common bandit by some and a brave revolutionary by others, Juan Cortina is one of the most fascinating characters in the 19th-century Southwest.

Recalling the Facts

Choose each correct answer and write the letter in the space provided.

_____ 1. Juan Cortina was called the "Red Robber" because he
  a. was a Communist.
  b. had a red beard.
  c. always dressed in red.

_____ 2. Cortina shot a marshal who was beating
  a. a fellow Mexican.
  b. a rich farmer.
  c. an old woman.

_____ 3. The Texas town Cortina's band took over was
  a. San Antonio.
  b. Brownsville.
  c. El Paso.

_____ 4. In his native state, Cortina served as
  a. mayor.
  b. captain.
  c. governor.

_____ 5. Juan Cortina was finally arrested for
  a. cattle rustling.
  b. murder.
  c. kidnapping.

_____ 6. Many poor Mexican Americans looked on Cortina as a
  a. bandit.
  b. hero.
  c. comic character.

The Arts and Technology

The Jacal and the Mano and Metate. This photograph shows Mexican Americans living in Texas in the 1880s. Their house is called a **jacal.** They made corn meal flour by grinding corn between two stones. The top stone is called a **mano.** The bottom one is a **metate.**

1. This one-hundred-year-old photo shows that a *jacal* was made out of what kinds of building materials? _____

_____

2. List three other things you can learn about this family's daily life by studying this photograph. _____

_____

Critical Thinking helps you think about what you have read and puts the chapter into historical perspective.

CHAPTER REVIEW: CRITICAL THINKING ▐

A **hypothesis** is a guess that you make because it seems likely to be true. When you make a guess, you try to find evidence to support it. Read the following paragraph. Then answer the questions.

After nearly 300 years of living in the Southwest, many Mexican Americans suddenly found themselves without land or power. They were often in conflict with the Anglos who had moved into the area.

1. How might the lives of Mexican Americans have been different in the Southwest if Anglo Americans had treated them fairly? Support your hypothesis. _____

_____

2. Other than violence, what ways might Mexican Americans have used to win their rights during this time? Support your hypothesis. _____

_____

The square indicates that you
have completed the chapter. **5** ■

Chapter 2 — THE SPANISH-AMERICAN WAR

AIM: Why did Spain and the United States go to war in 1898? How did the war's outcome affect Cuba and Puerto Rico?

1. Several hundred thousand Cubans died during the 1800s while trying to free Cuba from Spain. After the Cuban rebels failed to win the Ten Years' War against Spain in 1878, a new revolution was planned. Its new leader, José Martí, lived in New York from 1881 to 1895. Martí's skills as a journalist, poet, writer, and teacher helped him get support for his plans. By 1895, war broke out again between Cuban rebels and Spain. Martí left the United States. He was one of the first Cubans to die in the Revolution of 1895.

2. United States leaders watched the continuing struggle with growing concern. Americans had about $50 million invested in Cuba. They also carried on about $100 million a year in trade with Cuba. Both Cuban rebels and Spanish troops were killing civilians and burning property. American newspapers that favored war with Spain reported the terrible conditions under Spanish rule. United States President William McKinley sent the battleship *Maine* to Cuba to protect American citizens and property. In February 1898, the *Maine* mysteriously exploded in Havana harbor. Over 260 Americans on board were killed. The United States government blamed Spain.

3. The United States declared war on Spain in April 1898. In June, about 17,000 American troops landed at the southeastern tip of Cuba near the city of Santiago. Cuban soldiers led by General Calixto García joined up with the Americans. Together they attacked the Spanish near San Juan Hill, outside Santiago. One famous group of American fighters was the **Rough Riders,** with Theodore Roosevelt second in command. The Rough Riders included Hispanic Americans such as Captain Maximiliano Luna, whose family had lived in the Southwest since the 1650s.

4. The war was a short one. Within a few days American ships had destroyed the Spanish fleet in Santiago harbor. The Spanish troops in the city surrendered. Next, American troops landed in Puerto Rico and quickly captured the island from Spain. The 1898 peace treaty between Spain and the United States put an end to almost all of Spain's colonial empire. The treaty granted Cuba its freedom from Spain. The United States gained Guam, the Philippine Islands in the Pacific Ocean, and Puerto Rico.

5. The United States claimed that the Cubans needed time to form their own government. In 1899, the United States set up a military government that lasted for three years. Americans helped improve health conditions and build roads, schools, and bridges.

6. Many Cubans and Americans saw the United States as taking the place of Spain instead of giving Cuba its freedom. In 1901, the United States Congress passed the **Platt Amendment.** The Cubans made the amendment part of their 1901 constitution. The Platt Amendment gave the United States the right to come into Cuba to maintain order and to preserve Cuban independence. The United States was given the right to have a naval base in Cuba.

▲ Captain Maximiliano Luna was among the Rough Riders' officers.

Understanding What You Have Read

Write the name of the person **next to** the statement that each might have made. Not all choices will be used.

Calixto García   William McKinley
Theodore Roosevelt   José Martí
Maximiliano Luna

_____ 1. I led the Cuban revolution against Spain in 1895.

_____ 2. I was a Hispanic-American Rough Rider during the Spanish-American War.

_____ 3. I was a general who led Cuban troops in eastern Cuba and helped defeat the Spanish.

_____ 4. I was president of the United States during the Spanish-American War.

Linking Past to Present

Political Rights in Puerto Rico. Once the Americans gained Puerto Rico from Spain did that island's people enjoy the same political rights that the United States citizens had? Such was not the case. Many Puerto Ricans regarded the first years of American control after the Spanish-American War of 1898 as a step backward. That was because, in 1897, Puerto Ricans had forced Spain to give them a great deal of self-government.

But in 1898, under American control, Puerto Ricans found their political life quite different from what they had expected. Instead of choosing their own governor, the United States president appointed him as well as other Puerto Rican officials. Puerto Ricans could vote for only some of the members of their law-making bodies. The 1900 **Foraker Act,** passed by the United States Congress, did allow a Puerto Rican representative to give speeches in the United States House of Representatives—but not to vote.

In 1917, the United States passed the **Jones Act.** That law made Puerto Rico a United States territory. The Jones Act allowed Puerto Ricans to elect their own senate. In addition, Puerto Ricans were granted United States citizenship. Until 30 years later, however, Puerto Ricans could not choose their own governors nor elect many other of their own officials.

1. Do you think Puerto Ricans were surprised to find themselves using United States money and stamps and having a United States president choose their governor after

   1898? Support your opinion. _____

   _____

   _____

2. When and how did Puerto Ricans gain United States citizenship? _____

   _____

   _____

Carlos Juan Finlay. Thousands of American, Cuban, and Spanish soldiers died in Cuba during the Spanish-American War. However, only a small number of them lost their lives in battle. Most of them died from a terrible disease called **yellow fever.** Yellow fever had been killing Cubans, other Latin Americans, and Americans in the southern part of the United States for many years. No one knew where the disease came from or how to prevent it.

No one, that is, except the Cuban doctor Carlos Juan Finlay. Finlay was born in Cuba and studied medicine in Philadelphia, Pennsylvania. In 1881, he first proposed his theory that yellow fever was spread by a certain kind of mosquito. Everyone laughed at Finlay's theory, but he refused to give up on his idea.

In 1900, Cuba was still under U.S. military rule. An American Yellow Fever Commission was sent to Havana to find the cause of this deadly disease. It was headed by United States Army doctor Major Walter Reed. Reed visited Dr. Finlay, about whose theory he had heard. Finlay showed Reed the records of his experiments.

Finlay also gave Reed some little black mosquito eggs. Finlay believed the eggs would help Reed to continue the experiments where he had left off. The American doctors watched the eggs hatch. Reed and his team used American soldiers as volunteers. When the soldiers were bitten by the mosquitoes, they came down with yellow fever. The commission had the proof it needed to convince the world that yellow fever was spread to humans by this mosquito—the *Stegomyia fasciata*. The mosquito is now called *Aëdes aegypti*.

The United States Army, under the direction of engineer William Gorgas, destroyed the swamps where the mosquitoes lived. With the mosquitoes killed, yellow fever disappeared. This all came about because of a brave Cuban doctor with a theory he developed in spite of ridicule.

Recalling the Facts

Match each name or date in Column A with the correct description in Column B. Write the correct letter in each blank.

Column A	Column B
_____ 1. 1900	**a.** year Finlay first stated his theory on yellow fever
_____ 2. Walter Reed	**b.** U.S. engineer who helped prevent yellow fever
_____ 3. 1881	**c.** what Finlay gave to Reed for experiments
_____ 4. mosquito eggs	**d.** head of the American Yellow Fever Commission
_____ 5. *Sgomyia fasciata*	**e.** year the American Yellow Fever Commission came to Cuba
_____ 6. William Gorgas	**f.** mosquito that spread yellow fever

Using Primary Sources

George Santayana, a famous philosopher and writer, was born in Spain in 1863. He moved with his family to the United States in 1872 and lived in Boston for most of the next 40 years. He taught as a professor at Harvard University. Below is a section of his long poem entitled "Spain in America: Written After the Destruction of the Spanish Fleet in the Battle of Santiago, in 1898."

How many **galleons** sailed to sail no more,

How many battles and how many slain,

Since first Columbus touched the Cuban shore,

Till Araucania felt the yoke of Spain!

What **mounting** miseries! What **dwindling** gain!

To **till** those **solitudes**, soon swept of gold,

And beat that **ardent** sun, across the **main**

Slaves must come writhing in the **festering hold**

Of galleys.—Poison works, though men be brave and bold.

Vocabulary

galleons sailing ships Spain used for war and trade   **slain** killed   **yoke** cruel rule
mounting growing   **dwindling** shrinking   **gain** profit   **till** farm
solitudes lonely places   **ardent** hot   **main** sea
festering hold the rotting cargo area below deck

1. Columbus first touched Cuban shores in 1492. How many years did Spain's rule of Cuba last? _____

2. After Spain took what gold there was in Cuba, Spain shipped slaves from Africa to Cuba to do what kind of work? _____

3. Do you think Santayana favored or opposed Spain's defeat in 1898? Use evidence from this poem to support your opinion. _____
_____

CHAPTER REVIEW: CRITICAL THINKING

When you read about almost any issue, you learn **different points of view**. It is important to know from where each point of view comes. Suppose that you were *one* of the following in 1898: a United States citizen, a Spanish subject in Spain, a Cuban, or a Puerto Rican. Briefly describe what your reaction might have been to the peace treaty after the Spanish-American War. Give reasons for your opinions.

_____
_____
_____
_____

HISPANIC IMMIGRATION

AIM: Why did so many Mexicans, Cubans, and Puerto Ricans immigrate to the United States in the 35 years before World War I?

1. The early 1880s saw the start of a great migration. Porfirio Díaz was president of Mexico from 1876 to 1911. He had strong control of the Mexican government until 1910. Under Díaz's iron hand, the rich became richer and the poor, poorer. Many Mexicans chose to move to the United States. Díaz was overthrown in 1911. Ten years of bloody revolution in Mexico followed. At times, the United States got involved in disputes with different sides in the Mexican fighting. For several months in 1914, American forces occupied the port of Veracruz. In 1916, Pancho Villa led some Mexican fighters in attacks across the border into New Mexico. American troops entered Mexico but failed to catch Villa. During these years, another million Mexicans fled to the United States.

2. There were plenty of jobs for the new immigrants in the American Southwest. Farm workers were needed to pick cotton and other crops. Railroad workers were needed to lay tracks for the Southern Pacific and Santa Fe Railroads. Workers were needed in the growing number of mines and factories. Within a few years, Mexican immigrants made up the major work force in all these industries.

3. Cubans also immigrated to the United States to find jobs and peace. The fight for Cuban independence from Spain in the late 1800s seriously damaged the cigar industry. Cuban producers, such as Vicente Martínez Ybor, moved their businesses to the United States. Here they could work in peace and provide better pay for their workers. Ybor settled in Tampa, Florida. There, he created Ybor City, a city within a city for his workers.

4. Puerto Ricans came to the United States for the same reasons as Mexicans and Cubans. After the Spanish-American War, Puerto Rico became a territory of the United States. A territory does not have the same rights as a state. American business people came to Puerto Rico. They made sugarcane the main cash crop. Puerto Rican workers were not paid as well as workers in the United States. They earned as little as 12 cents a day. Some Puerto Ricans chose to immigrate to California and Hawaii where the working conditions were better. Others settled in New York.

5. Many **Basques** came to the United States from Spain. The Basques have lived as sheep herders for centuries in the Pyrenees Mountains in Spain. Like the Cubans, Mexicans, and Puerto Ricans, the Basques wanted a better life. Hundreds of Basque sheep herdsmen settled in northern California, Oregon, and Idaho. Today, Boise, Idaho, has more Basques than any other American city.

6. This period of **immigration** was just the beginning. The immigration of Hispanics to the United States would continue throughout the twentieth century. Each of these Hispanic groups would make a unique contribution to the culture of the United States.

▲ Mexican refugees flee the violence of the revolution in Mexico.

Understanding What You Have Read

A. Fill in the best word or words from the list below to complete each sentence.

Cuban   Mexican   railroads   Benito Juárez   Porfirio Díaz
houses   sugarcane   New York   Idaho

1. One reason Mexicans moved to the United States was the harsh life under the Mexican president _____.

2. The Southwest needed the new migrants to help build _____.

3. _____ immigrants came to Florida to work in cigar factories.

4. _____ workers left Puerto Rico for better pay in the United States.

5. Basque sheep herdsmen immigrated to Oregon and _____.

B. In each of the sentences that follow, the underlined word or words make the sentence true or false. If the sentence is true, write **T** in the blank before it. If it is false, write the word or words that will make it true.

_____ 1. <u>Mexican</u> immigrants became a major part of the work force in the Southwest by 1900.

_____ 2. The Mexican Revolution lasted <u>five</u> years.

_____ 3. <u>Vicente Martínez Ybor</u> hired many Cubans to work for him in Tampa, Florida.

_____ 4. Puerto Rican workers were paid <u>well</u> when the Anglo sugarcane producers came to Puerto Rico.

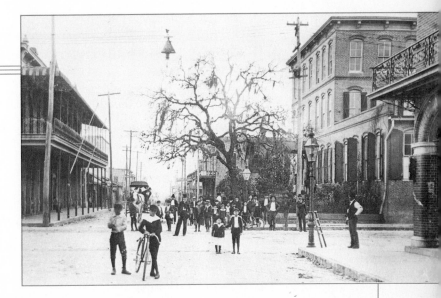

Daily Life

This photograph is of 14th Street and 9th Avenue in Ybor in the early 1900s. Many of the Cuban-American residents made their living by working in the cigar industry. They gathered on the street to listen to the Cuban revolutionary, José Martí. They also enjoyed deviled crabs and Cuban coffee sold by the street vendors.

1. What means of transportation were used in Ybor City? _____

2. Do the streets look similar to those of today? _____

   How are they different? _____

3. What were the buildings primarily made of? _____

Spotlight on People

Narciso Gener Gonzales. Few journalists in American history have matched Narciso Gener Gonzales's reputation as a crusader. Gonzales was the founder and first editor of *The State*, a daily newspaper in South Carolina's capital, Columbia.

Gonzales's father, Ambrosio Gonzales, was born in Cuba. He became a general in the Cuban revolutionary army during the 1840s. After the revolution General Gonzales migrated to the United States. He married the daughter of a wealthy Southern planter and author. Gonzales was born in 1858. By age 18, he was already a well-

known news reporter. He soon became the leading correspondent for the Charleston *News and Courier.*

In 1891, Narciso Gonzales founded *The State.* He promised the people that his paper would be "independent in its judgment and its utterances." In his editorials he condemned child labor and lynching of blacks. He spoke out for the women's right to vote and called for the improvement of city streets. He also attacked dishonest politicians. One of the worst of these was South Carolina's Lieutenant Governor Jim Tillman.

When Tillman ran for governor in 1902, Gonzales exposed his dishonest practices. Tillman lost the election and blamed Gonzales and his paper for his defeat. One day, six months later, Tillman met Gonzales on a busy street and shot him. There were many witnesses. Gonzales died four days later.

In Tillman's trial the jury found the shooting "justifiable." The jury said that Tillman believed Gonzales had hurt Tillman's reputation. Tillman was found innocent and freed from jail.

Recalling the Facts

Choose each correct answer and write the letter in the space provided.

_____ 1. Narciso Gener Gonzales's father was a general in
  a. Mexico.
  b. the Confederate army.
  c. Cuba.

_____ 2. The newspaper Gonzales founded was
  a. *The State.*
  b. *The News and Courier.*
  c. *The Morning Telegraph.*

_____ 3. In editorials, Gonzales condemned
  a. women's fight for the vote.
  b. all Southern politicians.
  c. lynchings.

_____ 4. Jim Tillman was South Carolina's
  a. lieutenant governor.
  b. governor.
  c. secretary of state.

_____ 5. Gonzales used his newspaper to explain
  a. why he wanted to run for governor.
  b. Tillman's qualifications for governor.
  c. Tillman's dishonest practices.

_____ 6. Tillman's shooting of Gonzales was an
  a. accident.
  b. act of revenge.
  c. act of cowardice.

The Arts and Technology

This song is a *corrido*. A corrido is a Mexican folk ballad about real events and legends. This corrido was sung by Mexicans as they left their homes and traveled north to a new life in the United States. The English words are on the right and the original Spanish, on the left.

¡Adios! mi Patria querida;
Yo ya me voy a ausentar;
Me voy para Estados Unidos,
Donde pienso trabajar.

Goodbye, my beloved country;
Now I'm going away;
I go to the United States,
Where I intend to work.

Me voy triste y pesaroso
A sufrir y a padecer;
Madre mía de Guadalupe,
Tú me concedas volver.

I go sad and heavy-hearted
To suffer and endure;
My Mother of Guadalupe,
Grant my safe return.

Pues yo no tengo la culpa
Que abandone así mi tierra;
La culpa es la pobreza
Que nos tiene en la miseria.

For I am not to blame
That I leave my country thus;
The fault is that of poverty,
Which keeps us all in need.

1. What is the mood of the singer as he or she leaves home? _____
   _____

2. What lines tell you the singer does not intend to stay in the United States? _____
   _____

3. Why does the singer have to go away? _____
   _____

CHAPTER REVIEW: CRITICAL THINKING

1. How did Hispanic Americans contribute to the growth and development of the Southwest?
   _____
   _____

2. What common reasons did Hispanics have for leaving their homelands? _____
   _____

Chapter 4

WORLD WAR I BRINGS CHANGES

AIM: What role did Hispanic Americans play in World War I? How did the war and its aftermath change their lives?

1. An event occurred in January 1917, that caused some Anglos to mistrust Mexican Americans. It also contributed to the United States entering World War I. A message was discovered called the **Zimmermann Note.** It was sent by Germany to Mexico. Germany was an enemy of the United States. The message asked the Mexicans to attack the United States if Germany and the United States went to war. In return, Germany promised that Mexico could reclaim the lands it had lost to the United States under the Treaty of Guadalupe Hidalgo. Mexico rejected Germany's offer. Mexican Americans remained patriotic and loyal to the United States.

2. The United States entered World War I in April 1917. The war affected all Americans, including **Hispanic Americans.** A large number of Hispanic Americans volunteered to join the armed forces. They were proud to serve their country in the war. Because they had fought so hard for their own freedom, they had a special reason to protect the freedom of the United States.

3. Hispanic Americans who did not fight in the war found new work opportunities. Many industries had lost workers who had gone to fight in the war. New workers were needed to take their places. Hispanic Americans were attracted by the better pay offered in factories in the Midwest and Northeast. By the end of the war in 1918, nearly 70,000 Hispanics had settled in large neighborhoods, called **colonias,** in cities east of the Mississippi River.

4. Returning Hispanic-American soldiers had learned many things from the war. They wanted a better life for themselves and their children. Many moved east. Others went to California. In California, there were more jobs than in the rest of the Southwest. By 1925, Los Angeles had more Mexican-born citizens than any other city except Mexico City. Chicago's Mexican American population grew to 20,000 by 1930. It was the largest Spanish-speaking area in the country outside of the Southwest.

5. Concerned about the large Mexican migration, the governor of California created a fact-finding committee in 1920 to learn about Hispanic Americans. The committee found that most Hispanic Americans had jobs and were doing well.

6. Hispanic Americans formed their own organizations to help each other in their new neighborhoods. Many had to adjust to living in cities. They also had to deal with **prejudice.** The first Mexican-American parish in Chicago was started in 1923. It was a place where Mexican Americans could come together to share their problems and hopes. By 1929, the parish, Nuestra Señora de Guadalupe, had 8,000 members. Thus the changes in the United States brought about by World War I brought new opportunities and concerns to Hispanic Americans.

▲ Women and men attend a language class in 1921 in San Antonio, Texas. What were some of the changes in the lives of Hispanic Americans after World War I?

Understanding What You Have Read

A. Place the events in the correct order by writing the numbers 1 through 5 in the blanks.

_____ a. Los Angeles has more Mexican Americans than any other United States city.

_____ b. Hispanic Americans move east looking for new jobs.

_____ c. The Zimmermann Note is discovered.

_____ d. Hispanic Americans enlist in the armed forces.

_____ e. The United States enters World War I.

B. Write the letter of the item in Column B that best describes each place in Column A.

Column A	Column B
_____ 1. *colonias*	a. United States enemy in World War I
_____ 2. Germany	b. home of the Hispanic-American Roman Catholic Church, Nuestra Señora de Guadalupe
_____ 3. California	c. country that was sent the Zimmermann note
_____ 4. Mexico	d. Hispanic-American neighborhoods in cities
_____ 5. Chicago	e. western state where many Hispanics went to live in the 1920s

Building Geography Skills

Study the map. Then answer the questions.

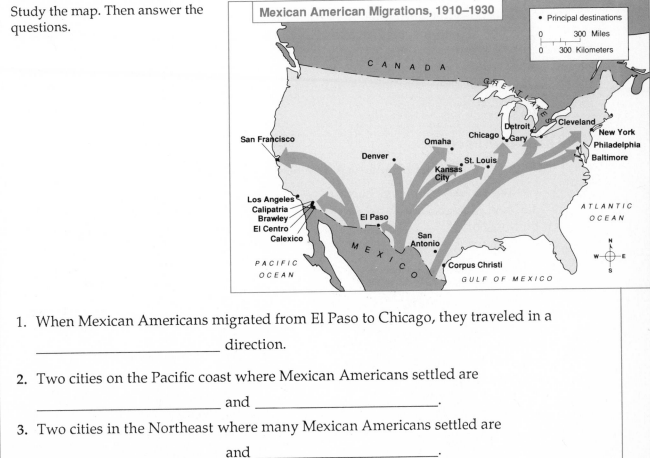

Mexican American Migrations, 1910–1930

1. When Mexican Americans migrated from El Paso to Chicago, they traveled in a
   _____ direction.

2. Two cities on the Pacific coast where Mexican Americans settled are
   _____ and _____.

3. Two cities in the Northeast where many Mexican Americans settled are
   _____ and _____.

Spotlight on People

Octaviano A. Larrazolo. When New Mexico became a state in 1912, a group of Hispanic-American leaders fought for the rights of their people. They made sure, in the new state **constitution,** that Hispanic Americans would have the right to hold political office. They also protected their right to vote. One leader of the group was Octaviano Larrazolo.

Larrazolo was born in Chihuahua, Mexico, in 1859. When he was just eleven years old, Larrazolo traveled to Tuscon, Arizona. There he saw Mexican Americans living in poverty. He vowed then that he would dedicate his life to helping his people. First he studied to be a priest. Later he added law to his education. His legal background helped him to build a career in politics. When New Mexico was still a territory, Larrazolo had been a candidate for delegate to the territorial legislature.

In 1916, Larrazolo became active in the election for New Mexico's second governor. The first governor of the state had been an Anglo American. Larrazolo wanted the next governor to be Hispanic American. He backed Ezequiel Cabeza de Baca for governor in 1916. De Baca had been a newspaper editor. He won the election but died of an illness only a month after he was in office.

A new election was held and Larrazolo decided to run for the office. He won the election. As governor he continued to have a special concern for the rights of Hispanic Americans. For example, he supported the teaching of Mexican-American culture and the use of both English and Spanish in the public schools. Larrazolo continued to be active in politics after his term as governor. In 1928, he was elected as one of New Mexico's senators in the United States Senate.

Recalling the Facts

Choose each correct answer and write the letter in the space provided.

_____ 1. Octaviano Larrazolo was born in
   a. New Mexico.
   b. Mexico.
   c. Arizona.

_____ 2. Larrazolo was educated in
   a. religion and medicine.
   b. medicine and law.
   c. religion and law.

_____ 3. In his childhood, Larrazolo was affected by seeing his people
   a. fight wars.
   b. living in poverty.
   c. moving away.

_____ 4. Larrazolo made sure that New Mexico's state constitution protected Hispanic American
   a. property.
   b. voting rights.
   c. segregation.

_____ 5. After Cabeza de Baca died in office, Larrazolo ran for
   a. governor.
   b. state senator.
   c. territorial delegate.

_____ 6. In 1928 Larrazolo became a
   a. governor.
   b. United States senator.
   c. judge.

The Arts and Technology

There are no statistics on the number of Hispanic Americans who served their country in World War I. We do know that many served bravely. Mexican Americans, from Texas, on their way to fight against Germany in France in 1918 sang this popular song.

Registration 1918

The cards arrived
at home for each one
verifying the registration
those twenty-one to thirty-one.

Good bye Laredo highlighted
by your towers and bells
but we shall never forget
your beautiful Mexican women.

They are taking us to fight
to some distant land
and taking us to fight
the German troops.

They are taking is to fight
in distinct directions
and taking us to fight
with different nations.

How far is the journey
over the waves
great will be my pleasure
if I will triumph.

When I was fighting
I would remember everybody
and more of my poor mother
that cried so much for me.

Good bye dear parents
and the lady I love
when we are in France
a sigh will send you.

Good bye Laredo highlighted
by your towers and bells
but we shall never forget your beautiful
Mexican women.

1. What are the "cards" referred to in the first stanza? _____

2. What mixed feelings do the soldiers singing this song have about their journey to

   France? _____

   _____

CHAPTER REVIEW: CRITICAL THINKING

If your shoelace is untied, it may cause you to trip. If you trip, it is the effect, or result, of the untied shoe. Recognizing **causes and effects** can help you understand history.

Life for Hispanic Americans changed after World War I. Many moved into the mainstream of American life.

1. In what ways, do you think, did World War I help Hispanic-American soldiers see the

   world differently? _____

   _____

2. Many Hispanic Americans had to adjust to factory work and city life in the East. What other

   things do you think they had to adjust to? _____

   _____

UNIT 1 REVIEW

Summary of the Unit

A few of the most important events and facts presented in Unit 1 are listed below. On a separate sheet of paper, copy these four and write four more.

1. Many Mexican Americans lost their land, wealth, and social position to Anglo Americans who migrated to the Southwest after the Civil War.
2. Cuba and Puerto Rico were freed from Spanish rule when Spain was defeated in the Spanish-American War.
3. Hispanics immigrated to the United States from 1880 to 1920 because of poverty and political unrest at home.
4. Hispanic Americans served their new nation loyally and bravely in World War I.

Understanding What You Have Read

Choose each correct answer and write the letter in the space provided.

_____ 1. The Treaty of Guadalupe Hidalgo gave the United States one-third of the land of
   a. California.
   b. Mexico.
   c. New Mexico.

_____ 2. Mexican bandits became famous for their attacks on
   a. poor Mexicans.
   b. Native Americans.
   c. Anglo Americans.

_____ 3. One cause of the Spanish-American War was
   a. the discovery of gold in Cuba.
   b. the explosion of a U.S. battleship.
   c. the revolt of slaves in Puerto Rico.

_____ 4. Mexicans did *not* immigrate to the United States because of
   a. a failed sugarcane crop.
   b. the Mexican Revolution.
   c. the dictator Porfirio Díaz.

_____ 5. The Zimmermann Note resulted in many Americans unfairly thinking Mexican Americans were
   a. patriotic.
   b. foolish.
   c. untrustworthy.

_____ 6. In the 1920s, many Mexican Americans moved to the
   a. Northwest.
   b. Midwest.
   c. Southeast.

Building Your Vocabulary

Complete each of the following sentences. Then find each word in the word puzzle. The hidden words are spelled from top to bottom, left to right, and diagonally (from corner to corner). Circle the words as you find them. The first one has been done for you.

_____ 1. A person who leaves one country and moves to another is an _____.

_____ 2. A Mexican folk ballad about real events or legends is called a _____.

_____ 3. The part of a southwestern U.S. town where Mexican Americans live is a _____.

_____ 4. Wealthy Mexican Americans were sometimes called _____.

_____ 5. People who live in the Pyrenees between France and Spain are _____.

_____ 6. Yellow fever is spread by a _____.

_____ 7. Puerto Ricans were given U.S. citizenship by the _____ Act.

_____ 8. Some of the Hispanic-American neighborhoods in cities are called _____.

```
A  R  I  C  O  S  F  J  C  O  J
B  W  T  M  K  R  P  D  O  N  T
A  A  S  O  M  B  O  V  L  C  V
R  B  S  S  L  I  Y  E  O  G  Q
R  H  A  Q  U  Z  G  O  N  T  I
I  P  C  U  U  M  R  I  Z  E  E
O  L  I  I  D  E  L  S  A  E  N
M  L  G  T  F  T  S  F  S  N  L
G  Q  J  O  N  E  S  E  Y  A  T
X  W  B  U  K  T  R  O  O  S  X
C  O  R  R  I  D  O  I  H  S  A
```

Developing Ideas and Skills—Using Maps

Study the map. Then answer the questions.

1. What two Caribbean islands were invaded by American troops in the Spanish-American War?

   _____

   _____

2. Near what city did most of the fighting in the Caribbean occur?

   _____

3. What Cuban patriot helped the Americans in the Spanish-American War?

   _____

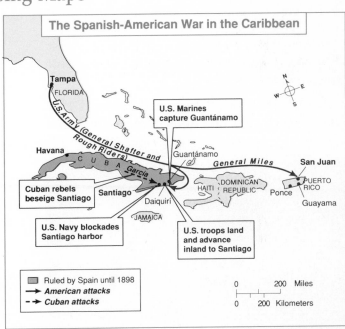

The Spanish-American War in the Caribbean

Tampa
FLORIDA
U.S. Army (General Shafter and Rough Riders)
U.S. Marines capture Guantánamo
Havana
CUBA
Garcia
Guantánamo
General Miles
San Juan
DOMINICAN REPUBLIC
HAITI
PUERTO RICO
Ponce
Cuban rebels beseige Santiago
Santiago
Daiquirí
Guayama
JAMAICA
U.S. Navy blockades Santiago harbor
U.S. troops land and advance inland to Santiago

▢ Ruled by Spain until 1898
→ American attacks
-→ Cuban attacks

0   200 Miles
0   200 Kilometers

Making History Live

1. Often myths grow up around important historical events. To find out the facts, research from several different sources has to be done. Write a brief report on the Rough Riders and the Battle of San Juan Hill. Describe the role of American troops, including Hispanic American troops, Cuban troops, and Spanish troops. Use several books in gathering information.

2. When different immigrant groups came to the United States, they brought their favorite recipes and ways of preparing food with them. Select three popular Hispanic-American foods and make drawings to show how they are prepared. You can research this by conducting interviews about food preparation with relatives or neighbors, by reading food labels in a food store, or by using a cookbook from a library.

Chapter 5 THE GREAT DEPRESSION

AIM: How did the Great Depression affect Hispanic Americans?

1. In 1929, the stock market crashed. That crash made many people who had invested money in the stock market instantly poor. It put millions of people out of work. The United States entered the Great Depression.

2. Many Mexican Americans lost their jobs during the Great Depression. In the early years of the depression, some Mexican Americans chose to go back to Mexico to look for work there. Like many other Americans, they had lost their jobs. They packed all their belongings into their cars or trucks and left. Most of these Mexican Americans were from the Southwest. But some were from the Great Lakes region and the East.

3. By 1931, negative feelings toward Hispanic Americans and other ethnic groups had grown. The secretary of labor in Washington, D.C. believed that **aliens**, foreigners living in one country while citizens of another country, should leave the United States. Then, other Americans could have their jobs and the Great Depression would end sooner.

4. The federal government began the Repatriation Program, an anti-alien drive. **Repatriation** means sending people back to their native land. The repatriation program was aimed especially at Mexican Americans in southern California. The Los Angeles County welfare officials offered free train rides back to Mexico from March 1931 to April 1934.

5. Between 1929 and 1939, about half of the three million Mexican Americans in the United States went to Mexico. Many left out of fear. Others were forced to leave. Even those who had become United States citizens felt pressured to leave.

6. During the **Great Depression,** wages were cut for workers who were lucky enough to have jobs. Wages for farm workers dropped from an average of 42 cents an hour in 1931 to 15 cents an hour in 1933. While President Roosevelt's **New Deal** legislation was helping urban workers, there was no relief for farm laborers.

7. Many strikes took place in California and Texas in the 1930s because of poor wages. The unions became stronger. The 1933 berry strike in El Monte, California, strengthened the newly formed union, La Confederación de Uniones de Campesinos y Obreros del Estado de California. The strikers gained higher wages and a shorter workday. The success of the berry strike led to strikes by the onion, celery, and cotton workers.

8. By the late 1930s, the United States economy became stronger. The repatriation program ended. Mexican Americans who were not happy in Mexico began returning to the United States. Labor unions were helping many American workers to earn a better living. The Great Depression was over.

▲ These women shelled pecans by hand. Why did workers such as these strike during the 1930s?

Understanding What You Have Read

In each of the sentences that follow, the underlined word or words make the sentence true or false. If the sentence is true, write **T** in the blank before it. If it is false, write the word or words in the blank that will make it true.

_____ 1. The stock market crash of 1929 led to the <u>Great Depression</u>.

_____ 2. Ethnic groups were <u>protected</u> by the federal government during the Great Depression.

_____ 3. Most Mexican Americans <u>voluntarily</u> went back to Mexico during the repatriation program.

_____ 4. The berry strike took place in <u>El Monte</u> , California.

_____ 5. La Confederación de Uniones de Campesinos y Obreros del Estado de California helped agricultural workers get <u>better</u> wages.

Daily Life

One of the factory jobs many Mexican Americans had was shelling pecans. In 1938, the pecan shellers in San Antonio, Texas, went on strike for better wages and working conditions. A Mexican-American women's organization wanted to help the strikers. They prepared tortillas and fed more than 1,000 strikers.

1. The picture shows some of the women who helped the strikers. What are these women doing? _____

_____

2. Why did the pecan shellers go on strike? _____

Dennis Chávez. In 1888, Dennis Chávez was born into a poor Mexican-American family outside of Albuquerque, New Mexico. He had to leave school at the age of 13 to work. He educated himself by reading books. He became involved in politics and had an opportunity to work in Washington, D.C. While at the nation's capital, Chávez put himself through Georgetown University.

Chávez returned to New Mexico after graduating and entered local politics. He was elected to that state's lawmaking body. In 1930, he was elected to the first of two terms in the United States House of Representatives. Then he tried for a Senate seat.

The 1934 Senate election in New Mexico was a close one. Bronson Cutting, the Republican candidate, beat Democrat Dennis Chávez by only 1,261 votes. Chávez thought that the election results were suspicious. He petitioned the United States Senate to remove Cutting from office.

Chávez's challenge of Bronson Cutting's Senate seat had an unexpected outcome. In 1935, Cutting died suddenly in an airplane crash before the Senate could vote on Chávez's petition. Chávez was appointed in Cutting's place as senator until the next election. In 1936, the people of New Mexico elected Chávez by a large margin.

Senator Chávez was a champion of Hispanic-American rights during the depression. He supported the New Deal programs of President Franklin Roosevelt. He served New Mexico faithfully in the Senate until his death in 1962. In the Capitol building in Washington, D.C. there stands a statue of Dennis Chávez, representing the state he loved so much.

Recalling the Facts

Match each person, date, or place in Column A to the words that identify it in Column B. Write the correct letter of your answer in each blank.

Column A	Column B
_____ 1. 1934	a. the Republican senator from New Mexico
_____ 2. Bronson Cutting	b. Dennis Chávez's hometown
_____ 3. Washington, D.C.	c. location of statue of Chávez
_____ 4. Franklin Roosevelt	d. year Chávez won first term to House of Representatives
_____ 5. Albuquerque	e. the president Senator Chávez served under
_____ 6. 1930	f. the year Chávez first ran for Senate

Using Primary Sources

The **barrio** could be a place of sadness and grief. However, it could also a place of happiness and fond memories. Below are the childhood memories of Henry García. García is a Mexican American who grew up in Barrio El Hoyo in Tuscon, Arizona, in the 1920s and 1930s.

> I was born on Meyer Street in 1921. We lived on Meyer Street in an area that was called El Corral. At first we had our home right where our business was, but in 1923 my parents built a house in the barrio called El Hoyo. Our house was built of **adobe** [sun-dried bricks of dirt and clay], of course.
>
> Now that I remember, the life in those old barrios was a full and rich one. We all lived together—there was a mixture of people—Jews, Syrians, naturally many Mexicans, Chinese, Lebanese—and everyone spoke Spanish.
>
> . . . In those days we all lived close together—one house was right next to the other and women visited over the fence. A boy could have a lot of adventures. I saw a lot of things and learned a lot. There were a lot of fiestas. Anytime there was a baptism or birthday there was a fiesta. There was always music. . . . The fiestas and dances were held in the yards of the houses. They would water down the patios and put up strings of lights. Then the musicians would arrive and the people of the barrio would come together.
>
> —from *Images and Conversations: Mexican Americans Recall a Southwestern Past*, University of Arizona Press © 1983 by Patricia Preciado Martin, pp. 69–71.

1. What things about barrio life would you like to have experienced?_____

_____

2. Why, do you think, did Henry García remember life in the barrios as "full and rich"?

_____

_____

CHAPTER REVIEW: CRITICAL THINKING

When you **infer** something, you figure it out. To make an inference, you use what you already know to explain something else.

1. Why did labor unions become strong during this period? _____

_____

2. How do you think the Mexican government and the Mexican people reacted to the flow of more than a million Mexican Americans back to Mexico from 1929 to 1939? Explain why.

_____

_____

Chapter 6 WORLD WAR II

AIMS: What role did Hispanic Americans play during World War II? How were they treated at home during the war?

1. On December 7, 1941, the Japanese bombed Pearl Harbor in Hawaii in a surprise attack. The United States Pacific naval fleet was stationed there. On December 8, the United States declared war on Japan. The United States had entered World War II.

2. Almost 400,000 Hispanic Americans served in the armed forces in World War II. A higher percentage of Hispanic Americans saw combat duty overseas than any other ethnic group in the United States. They also received more military medals than any other ethnic minority in the United States.

3. For many Hispanic Americans, the war was their first chance to experience life outside their neighborhoods. They were welcomed as soldiers in Europe. When they returned home they wanted a better life. However, at home they still experienced **discrimination**. Hispanic-American soldiers returning to the United States might be refused service in a restaurant, for example.

▲ Technical Sergeant Cleto Rodriguez of San Antonio, Texas, received the Congressional Medal of Honor for his brave fighting in the Philippines during World War II.

4. Twelve Hispanic-American soldiers earned the **Congressional Medal of Honor** during World War II. It was the highest military honor. One of those honored was José López of Brownsville, Texas. During the Normandy invasion in France in 1944, López held back a German counterattack. He did it with almost no support from retreating American troops.

5. World War II brought new opportunities for Hispanic Americans on the home front too. Many white male factory workers became soldiers. Women and ethnic groups who had been denied factory work were suddenly in great demand. Hispanic American farm workers moved to the cities to take factory jobs. Meanwhile in July 1942, the *bracero* program began. The **bracero program** was an agreement between the United States and Mexico. It encouraged braceros, Mexican farm workers, to work in the United States. It was a major contribution by Mexico to aid the war effort.

6. In some American cities, the increase in the Hispanic-American population led to conflict. The Sleepy Lagoon case in Los Angeles is one example. The Sleepy Lagoon was a gravel pit where Hispanic Americans swam. They could not use the public swimming pool. On August 2, 1942, José Díaz was found unconscious near Sleepy Lagoon. He died soon after he was discovered. Twenty-four Mexican American youths were arrested and charged with Díaz's death.

7. The trial caused further problems. The judge refused to allow the youths to change their clothes or cut their hair before going on trial. Twelve of the twenty-four were found guilty. But in October 1944, the verdict was reversed by a higher court for lack of evidence. The Sleepy Lagoon case sparked violence between Mexican-American gangs and Anglos in Los Angeles.

8. Despite problems, by 1945 many Hispanic Americans were better off economically. They also expected full recognition as equal Americans because of their role in the war.

Understanding What You Have Read

Write the best word or words from the list below to complete each sentence.

José López   braceros   Pearl Harbor
factories   Medal   discrimination

1. The United States became involved in World War II because the Japanese

   bombed _____ .

2. In 1944 _____ held back a German attack during the Normandy invasion.

3. Twelve Hispanic Americans received the Congressional _____ of Honor for their bravery in battle.

4. During World War II, Hispanic Americans found plenty of jobs in war production

   _____ .

5. The _____ program allowed Mexicans to enter the United States during World

   War II to provide farm labor.

6. The Sleepy Lagoon case was one example of _____ toward Hispanic Americans in the 1940s.

Daily Life

In the 1930s and 1940s, Hispanic-American women found new kinds of work. In the 1930s, many began to work in the garment factories. The garment factories were located mostly in large cities in the Southwest. These women made up 50 to 75 percent of the garment workers. Some of the women were the main income earners for their families. These women were paid very low wages, and they worked long hours in the hot, noisy factories. They organized into **labor unions** to improve working conditions.

In the 1940s, many Hispanic American women were able to find jobs in factories and war-related industry. That was because the men were in the armed forces.

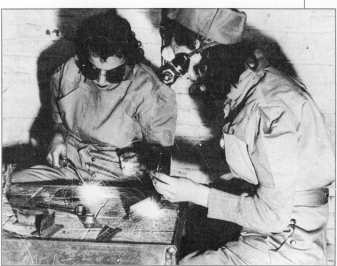

▲ These Hispanic-American women obtained gas-welding jobs during World War II.

1. Why did it become necessary for Hispanic-American garment workers to join labor

   unions? _____

   _____

2. Why were more Hispanic-American women able to find factory jobs in the 1940s?

   _____

   _____

Lucrezia Bori. On December 24, 1888, a baby girl was born in Valencia, Spain. Her name was Lucrezia Bori. She was to become a well-known and popular opera singer at the Metropolitan Opera in New York City.

Bori studied to become a singer in Milan, Italy. Her first performance was in an Italian theater on October 31, 1908. Her first performance in the United States was four years later at the Metropolitan Opera. Americans cheered her performance.

Lucrezia Bori spent almost 15 years working at the Metropolitan Opera—from 1921 to 1936. When the Metropolitan Opera faced economic problems during the Great Depression, she helped to save it. Bori became chairperson of the Save the Metropolitan Opera committee. A large amount of money was raised.

Bori's last performance at the Metropolitan was on March 21, 1936. The opera was *La Rondine*. After her successful opera singing career had ended, Bori remained active. She was the first woman opera singer to be elected a member of the board of directors of the Metropolitan Opera. She served on the board throughout the rest of the 1930s, through the World War II period, and up to her death in 1960.

Recalling the Facts

Choose each correct answer and write the letter in the space provided.

_____ 1. Lucrezia Bori was born in
   a. Cuba.
   b. Spain.
   c. Mexico.

_____ 2. Bori became famous as a (an)
   a. rock singer.
   b. blues singer.
   c. opera singer.

_____ 3. Bori spent the greatest part of her career working
   a. at the Metropolitan Opera.
   b. at La Scala.
   c. in Spain.

_____ 4. Bori helped save the Metropolitan Opera by
   a. standing in picket lines.
   b. rebuilding it.
   c. raising money for it.

_____ 5. March 21, 1936, was the date of
   a. Bori's first performance.
   b. Bori's last performance.
   c. Bori's becoming a member of the Metropolitan Opera's board of directors.

Using Primary Sources

During World War II, there were strong national feelings in the United States. Often, ethnic groups were considered outsiders and they were discriminated against. Fights often broke out between Mexican American youths and Anglo servicemen who came on leave to Los Angeles.

The headlines above actually appeared in newspapers of the time. (Note: A **zoot suit** is a style of suit popular among Mexican-American youths at that time.) A major riot took place on June 7, 1943, when thousands of sailors attacked Mexican-American youths in Los Angeles.

1. Why do you think Anglos considered ethnic groups outsiders during World War II?

    _____

    _____

2. Whom do the headlines imply are to blame for the fights? _____

    _____

CHAPTER REVIEW: CRITICAL THINKING

Answer the following questions which will aid you in **drawing conclusions** about events during World War II.

1. What kinds of changes did World War II bring to Hispanic Americans?

    _____

    _____

2. During World War II, the 295th Infantry regiment from Puerto Rico was on active duty in the Caribbean. Find the Caribbean islands on a world map. Why was the Caribbean an

    important area to protect and defend? _____

    _____

Chapter 7 PROGRESS AFTER WORLD WAR II

AIM: How did the lives of Hispanic Americans change after World War II?

1. After World War II many Hispanic Americans had a new outlook on their place in America. Returning soldiers and sailors had just fought against Hitler's racism. Hispanic Americans wanted to fight discrimination and racism at home. The **G.I. Bill of Rights** helped some Hispanic-American service people with job training, education, and loans. However, many Hispanic Americans still had to fight for equal opportunities in jobs, education, housing, and politics.

2. Some Hispanic Americans used politics as a way to voice their concerns about Hispanic problems. Edward Roybal was a Mexican American from Los Angeles. In 1948, he worked with the Community Service Organization (CSO). The CSO was a grass roots political movement to encourage Hispanics to vote. The CSO registered 12,000 new Hispanic voters in Los Angeles its first year. In the 1949 local elections, Roybal won a seat on the Los Angeles City Council by 8,000 votes. By being in government, he could voice the concerns of Mexican Americans in his community.

3. War surgeon Héctor García formed the American G.I. Forum after the war. This group's aim was to defend the civil rights of Mexican Americans. Its special interest was the rights of war veterans and their families. The organization fought discrimination in housing, education, and employment.

4. Molly C. Galván became a leader in the G.I. Forum. She organized a local Forum group in Salt Lake City, Utah. Then she became a national organizer. In 1957, she won a scholarship to study race relations at Fisk University in Tennessee. After that, Galván traveled throughout the United States working for better race relations.

5. Before the war, Hispanic Americans had used union strikes to improve their wages and working conditions. After the war, however, the unions were weakened. The bracero program, started during the war, continued. Whenever farm workers went on strike, braceros from Mexico were hired to do the work. Sometimes braceros were paid more than the farm workers had been paid.

6. Puerto Ricans believed strongly in the freedoms that they had fought for during World War II. Those freedoms included the right of self-government. After the war, Puerto Rico·worked to improve its industry and to gain independence from the United States. The 1917 Jones Act had made Puerto Ricans citizens of the United States. In 1947, the United States Congress amended the Jones Act. Now Puerto Ricans could elect their own governor. This amendment was an important step in Puerto Rico's fight for self-government.

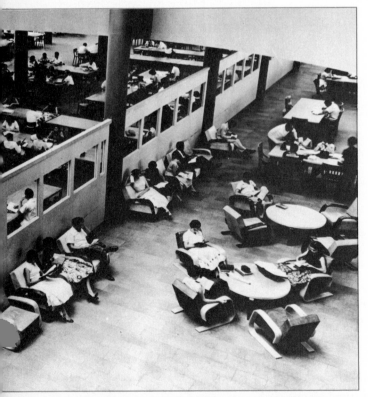

▲ Students read in the library at the University of Puerto Rico in the 1950s. THe G.I. Bill helped some Hispanic Americans pay for their higher education.

Match each word or words in column A with the correct explanation in column B. Write the letter of the correct answer in each blank.

Column A	Column B
_____ **1.** G.I. Bill of Rights	**a.** group that helped to register voters
_____ **2.** Molly Galván	**b.** Hispanic-American group that settled mostly in New York City
_____ **3.** American G.I. Forum	**c.** a program that gave job training and educational opportunities to World War II veterans
_____ **4.** braceros	**d.** organized a G.I. Forum in Salt Lake City
_____ **5.** Puerto Ricans	**e.** Mexican workers who helped to weaken the unions
_____ **6.** Community Service Organization	**f.** organization that worked for the civil rights of Hispanic Americans

Building Geography Skills

Study the following graph that shows how many braceros entered the United States between 1946 and 1962. (The bracero program actually ended in 1964.) Then write the correct answer to each question below.

1. How many braceros came to the United States in

   1946? _____

2. In which year shown did the largest number of braceros come to the

   United States?_____

3. What happened to the bracero program between

   1958 and 1962? _____

   _____

   _____

   _____

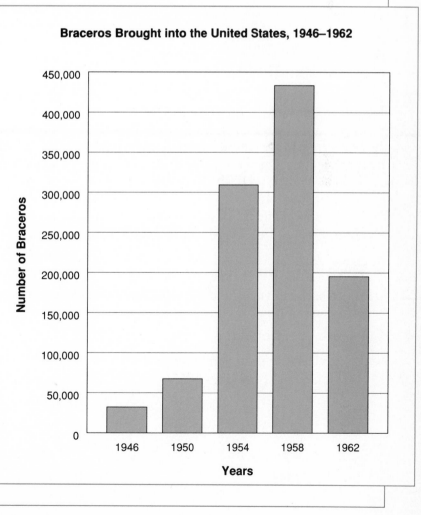

Braceros Brought into the United States, 1946–1962

Spotlight on People

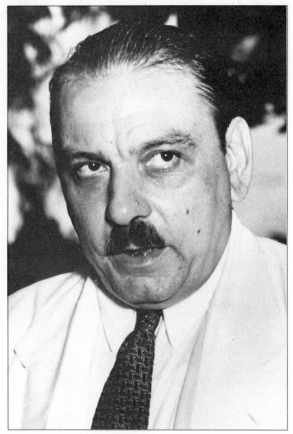

Luis Muñoz Marín. The year 1898 is an important date for Puerto Ricans. It is the year the United States gained the island from Spain. It is also the birthday of Luis Muñoz Marín, who showed them how to use that freedom.

Muñoz spent most of his youth in the United States. In 1910, Marín and his family moved from New York City to Washington, D.C., and Muñoz Marín went to Georgetown University.

In 1920, Muñoz returned to Puerto Rico. There he was elected to Puerto Rico's Senate. He fought hard for the interests of Puerto Rico's poor people. Also, he fought for Puerto Rico's independence from the United States in the 1930s.

During World War II, Marín started a program called **Operation Bootstrap.** This program encouraged Puerto Ricans to help themselves by improving health, education, and farming methods and creating new industry.

In 1949, Luis Muñoz Marín became Puerto Rico's first elected governor. As governor, Marín started Operation Commonwealth. Its goal was to achieve more self-rule from the United States. In 1952, Puerto Rico succeeded in becoming a **commonwealth** of the United States.

The last phase of Marín's great plan was called **Operation *Serenidad*** (Serenity). He felt that Puerto Ricans might enjoy life more if they could enjoy the arts. Operation *Serenidad* encouraged development and enjoyment of the arts in Puerto Rico.

In 1964, Muñoz Marín decided not to run for a fifth term as governor of Puerto Rico. Marín continued to contribute to Puerto Rico, however, by returning to his Senate seat. Muñoz Marín died in 1980.

Recalling the Facts

Match each term in column A to the words that identify it in column B. Write the correct letter of your answer in each blank.

Column A

_____ 1. Operation *Serenidad*

_____ 2. Luis Muñoz Marín

_____ 3. Operation Bootstrap

_____ 4. Operation Commonwealth

_____ 5. 1898

Column B

a. worked toward Puerto Rico's self-government

b. program that encouraged creativity in Puerto Ricans

c. the first elected governor of Puerto Rico

d. encouraged Puerto Ricans to help themselves

e. the year Puerto Rico won its independence from Spain

The Arts and Technology

Architecture. José Luis Sert was born in Barcelona, Spain. He studied to become an architect in Barcelona. In 1939, he moved to the United States and joined an American architect company. He worked on urban design for cities such as Rio de Janeiro and Bogotá. He also worked on the design of buildings on the Harvard University and Boston University campuses.

José Luis Sert's architectural ▶ office designed these buildings at Harvard University. In 1953, Sert was appointed dean of the Graduate School of Design and professor of architecture at Harvard University.

1. How would you describe Sert's style of architecture? _____

2. From which Spanish-speaking country did Sert come to the United States? _____

CHAPTER REVIEW: CRITICAL THINKING

You can summarize information, or write it in a few key sentences, to help you remember it. Reread paragraphs 2, 5, and 6. Then write a one- or two-line headline to summarize what you have read in each paragraph.

1. *Paragraph 2* _____

_____

2. *Paragraph 5* _____

_____

3. *Paragraph 6* _____

_____

Chapter 8 THE KOREAN AND VIETNAM WARS

AIM: What role did Hispanic Americans play in the Korean and Vietnam wars?

1. The wars in Korea and Vietnam affected the lives of all Americans. How did the United States get involved in the Korean War? In 1950, Communist soldiers from North Korea invaded South Korea. When the Communists refused to leave, 17 member countries of the United Nations sent troops to help the South Koreans. The United States provided most of the soldiers and supplies for South Korea. China and the Soviet Union supported the North Koreans.

2. As in earlier wars, thousands of Hispanic Americans fought bravely in Korea. One fighting unit, the 65th Infantry Regiment, was made up entirely of Puerto Ricans. They took part in nine major campaigns in Korea. A famous Hispanic-American war hero was flying ace

▲ The Congressional Medal of Honor is the United States's highest award for military bravery. It is awarded by the president in the name of Congress.

Colonel Manuel J. Fernández. He shot down many North Korean MIG planes and flew 125 combat missions. Nine Hispanic Americans were awarded Congressional Medals of Honor for their part in the Korean conflict. The war ended in 1953.

3. Within a few years the United States was fighting a war in Vietnam. In 1957, Communist rebels in South Vietnam had begun to fight the government of that tiny country. The rebels, or **Viet Cong,** were supported by the Communist government of North Vietnam. The United States went to the aid of South Vietnam. Again, many Hispanic Americans were drafted or joined the armed forces. One of them, Everett Álvarez, Jr., became the first prisoner taken in North Vietnam. Álvarez, a navy pilot, was shot down by the enemy in 1964. He was a prisoner of war for over eight years. Finally, in 1973, he was released and came home to California as a national hero.

4. Unfortunately, most returning Vietnam veterans did not receive a hero's welcome as in other wars. The war became unpopular with many Americans. They questioned the United States's right to be in Vietnam. There were many protests against the war. When they returned home, many veterans were rejected or ignored. Like many other veterans, Hispanic-American veterans had a hard time finding jobs. They were angry about the poor way they were treated. They were angry that so many of their fellow Hispanic Americans died in a war many people now said was wrong. Hispanic-American communities throughout the country suffered very high casualties (the number of wounded and killed) in the Vietnam War. For example, nearly a fifth of all soldiers from the Southwest who were wounded and killed were Hispanic Americans.

5. Many Americans, including Hispanic American veterans and their friends, demonstrated against the war. In 1973 , the United States withdrew American troops from the fighting.

Understanding What You Have Read

A. Place the name of **each person** below next to the statement that each might have made. There is one **extra name**.

Everett Álvarez, Jr.   Rubén Salazar   Manuel J. Fernández

_____ **1.** I was a prisoner of war in North Vietnam.

_____ **2.** I was a war hero in Korea.

B. Place the events below **in the correct** order by writing **the numbers** 1 through 6 in the blanks.

_____ **a.** The United Nations sends troops to South Korea.

_____ **b.** The Korean conflict ends.

_____ **c.** The United States withdraws from South Vietnam.

_____ **d.** The Viet Cong rebel against the South Vietnamese government.

_____ **e.** North Korea invades South Korea.

_____ **f.** Álvarez is taken prisoner of war.

Daily Life

Special Forces Camps in Vietnam. From 1961 to 1965, the United States set up over 80 Special Forces camps in South Vietnam. Each camp was a self-contained unit made up of both U.S. soldiers and South Vietnam minority groups. The job of the U.S. team was to advise and help the South Vietnamese in their war against the invading Communist fighters.

The camps were soon the target of Viet Cong attacks. In one surprise attack at Hiep Hoa in February 1963, Mexican-American Sergeant First Class Isaac Camacho became a hero. After being pinned down by Viet Cong gunfire, Camacho was separated from the other soldiers. The enemy captured him. He escaped almost 20 months later and crossed through miles of Communist territory to freedom. In September 1965, Camacho was awarded the Silver Star and Bronze Star medals for his bravery under attack and for his daring escape.

1. What was the purpose of the Special Forces camps? _____

_____

2. Why was Camacho awarded the Silver Star and Bronze Star medals? _____

_____

_____

3. How would you define the term *hero*? _____

_____

_____

Spotlight on People

Mercedes O. Cubría. Her official rank was major, but to hundreds of Cuban refugees she was simply *La Tía*—"the Aunt." The care and love she showed them went far beyond the call of duty.

Mercedes O. Cubría (1903–1980) was born in Guantánamo, Cuba. Her mother died when she was three. After this, she came to live in the United States with her two sisters. She worked as a nurse, interpreter, and rancher before joining the Women's Army Corps (WACs) in 1943. She became a second lieutenant and the first Cuban-born woman officer in the U.S. Army. During World War II she served as a codes officer in England, putting important government papers into a secret code. After the war, she was promoted to captain and then to major.

She served in Japan during the Korean War and was awarded the Bronze Star for her work as an **intelligence officer.** Such officers gather and study information about the country's enemies or possible enemies. Major Cubría retired from the army in 1953 due to illness. This was not to be the end of her military career, however.

She was recalled to active duty in 1962 at age 58. Cuba had undergone a Communist revolution. Thousands of Cubans had fled to the United States. Cubría's job was to interview these refugees and prepare reports on Cuba. In her spare time she helped the refugees find jobs and housing.

She retired for the second time in 1973, after being promoted to lieutenant colonel. She lived in Miami surrounded by friends and family until her death in 1980.

Recalling the Facts

Choose each correct answer and write the letter in the space provided.

_____ 1. Mercedes O. Cubría was the first
   a. woman army officer.
   b. Cuban-born, woman army officer.
   c. Spanish WAC.

_____ 2. Major Cubría retired in 1953 due to
   a. age.
   b. illness.
   c. marriage.

_____ 3. Her nickname, *La Tía*, means
   a. "the Aunt."
   b. "the Friend."
   c. "the Soldier."

_____ 4. In World War II, Mercedes Cubría's work involved
   a. combat training.
   b. supplies.
   c. codes.

_____ 5. She was returned to active duty in
   a. 1962.
   b. 1967.
   c. 1973.

_____ 6. Captain Cubría's job was to interview
   a. new soldiers.
   b. Communist prisoners.
   c. Cuban refugees.

Using Primary Sources

A total of 37 Hispanic Americans have been honored with the Congressional Medal of Honor in combat dating back to the U.S. Civil War. Below is the Medal of Honor citation for Luis Fernando García (1929–1952), a Marine private, born in Puerto Rico, who courageously gave his life for his country during the Korean War.

> For conspicuous gallantry [clear bravery] and intrepidity [fearlessness] at the risk of his life above and beyond the call of duty while serving as a member of company I, in action against aggressor [attacking] forces. . . . During a savage night attack . . . Pfc. [Private First Class] Garcia, although suffering painful wounds, moved though the intense [heavy] hail of hostile fire to a supply point to secure more hand grenades. Quick to act when a hostile grenade landed nearby, endangering the life of another marine, as well as his own, he unhesitatingly [without stopping] chose to sacrifice himself and immediately threw his body upon the deadly missile. His great personal valor and cool decision in the face of almost certain death sustain [keep up] and enhance [add to] the finest traditions of the U.S. Naval Service. He gallantly [bravely] gave his life for his country.

1. What was Luis García's final act of bravery? _____

   _____

2. What made García's act especially worthy of the Congressional Medal of Honor?

   _____

   _____

CHAPTER REVIEW: CRITICAL THINKING

You can **compare and contrast** different historical events to gain a better understanding of them. Hispanic Americans fought in the Korean and Vietnam wars. Some also protested the Vietnam War and took part in demonstrations against the war.

1. Compare and contrast how the Vietnam War differed from earlier wars that Hispanic

   Americans fought in. _____

   _____

2. Do you think that Hispanic Americans and other Vietnam War veterans had a right to react

   the way they did on their return home? Why or why not? _____

   _____

UNIT 2 REVIEW

Summary of the Unit

A few of the most important events and facts presented in Unit 2 are listed below. Write them in your notebook and add three more.

1. Many Hispanic Americans lost their jobs and were sent back to Mexico during the Great Depression.
2. Hispanic Americans served their country courageously in the armed forces in World War II.
3. During World War II, many Hispanic Americans moved to cities and found work in factories.
4. Hispanic Americans supported political groups and unions to improve their lives in the post–World War II years.
5. Hispanic Americans participated bravely in the Korean and Vietnam wars.

Understanding What You Have Read

Choose the word that best completes each sentence. Write the letter of your answer in the space provided.

_____ 1. Many people, including Mexican Americans, lost their jobs or received lower wages during
      a. World War I.   **b.** the Great Depression.   **c.** World War II.

_____ 2. To separate people according to their race or ethnic group is to
      a. segregate them.
      b. discriminate against them.
      c. deport them.

_____ 3. A Hispanic American who held back a German counterattack in Normandy with little help during World War II was
      a. Dennis Chávez.
      b. José López.
      c. Manuel J. Fernández.

_____ 4. A Mexican who came to the United States to work the fields during World War II was called a (an)
      a. citizen.   **b.** immigrant.   **c.** *bracero*.

_____ 5. The goal of the Community Services Organization was to get Hispanic Americans
      a. to register to vote.
      b. decent housing.
      c. citizenship.

_____ 6. Molly C. Galván worked to improve
      a. race relations.
      b. growers' rights.
      c. the *bracero* program.

_____ 7. A Hispanic-American flying ace in the Korean War was
      a. Isaac Camacho.
      b. Everett Alvarez, Jr.
      c. Manuel J. Fernández.

_____ 8. During the Korean War, Mercedes O. Cubría was
      a. an interpreter.   **b.** an intelligence officer.   **c.** a nurse.

Building Your Vocabulary

Choose the word or words from the list below that best complete each sentence. Write the word or words in the blank.

civil rights   prisoner of war   repatriation
governor   Congressional Medal of Honor   strike

1. In the 1930s, many young Hispanic Americans were sent to Mexico under the

   _____ program.

2. An important farm workers group was formed as a result of a 1933 _____ in California.

3. Seventeen Hispanic Americans in World War II received the _____.

4. The American G.I. Forum was formed to help Hispanic Americans protect their

   _____.

5. In 1947 Puerto Ricans gained the right to choose their own _____.

6. Everett Alvarez, Jr., became the first _____ during the Vietnam War.

Developing Ideas and Skills—Using Time Lines

Study the time line. Then write the letter of the correct choice in the space provided.

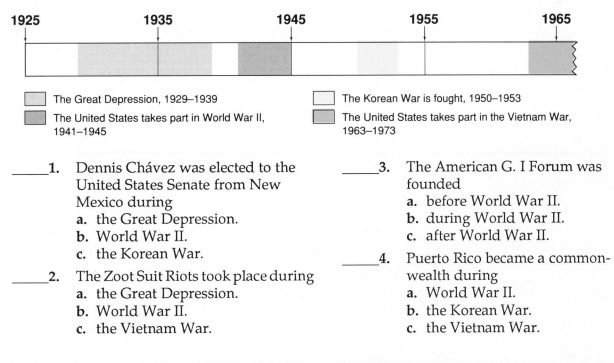

1925   1935   1945   1955   1965

- The Great Depression, 1929–1939
- The United States takes part in World War II, 1941–1945
- The Korean War is fought, 1950–1953
- The United States takes part in the Vietnam War, 1963–1973

_____ 1. Dennis Chávez was elected to the United States Senate from New Mexico during
    a. the Great Depression.
    b. World War II.
    c. the Korean War.

_____ 2. The Zoot Suit Riots took place during
    a. the Great Depression.
    b. World War II.
    c. the Vietnam War.

_____ 3. The American G. I Forum was founded
    a. before World War II.
    b. during World War II.
    c. after World War II.

_____ 4. Puerto Rico became a commonwealth during
    a. World War II.
    b. the Korean War.
    c. the Vietnam War.

Making History Live

1. Write a brief report explaining why it is important for all Americans to understand politics and use their voting power.

2. Write a brief report about one of the following topics. Use your school library or public library to help you get information for your report. Present your report to the class.
    a. American G. I. Forum
    b. Puerto Rico during the 1940s
    c. the repatriation program
    d. a key battle in World War II, the Korean War, or the Vietnam War

3. Make a drawing or painting showing an important event in the life of one of the following people: Dennis Chávez, Lucrezia Bori, Luis Muñoz Marín, Mercedes O. Cubría.

Chapter 9 THE CIVIL RIGHTS MOVEMENT

AIM: What gains did Hispanic Americans make in politics and the working place during the 1960s and 1970s?

1. The 1960s and 1970s were a time of great change for Hispanic Americans. One man who had a lot to do with the change was César Chávez. He was a Mexican-American farm worker. As a child, he saw his family lose their farm in the Great Depression and become poor **migrant farm workers.** Later, Chávez became a community organizer and then general director of the Community Service Organization, (CSO). In 1962, Chávez started the National Farm Workers Association (NFWA).

2. In 1965, **Chávez** called for a strike against the grape growers in Delano, California. He wanted better working conditions. The strike quickly spread throughout the state. The wine grape growers soon settled with the union. However, the growers of table grapes refused to give in to union demands. Strikers were arrested. Chávez received death threats. The strikers would not give up. In 1967, Chávez called for a national **boycott** of grapes. People all over the country stopped buying grapes. It was labor's first successful national boycott in American history.

3. The five-year strike finally ended in victory for the union, now called the United Farm Workers Organizing Committee (UFWOC). In 1966, Chávez's group had joined with a committee of the American Federation of Labor-Congress of Industrial Organizations (AFL-CIO). The union was now recognized by the growers. Hispanic Americans felt the power they could have when they joined together.

4. Other leaders appeared on the scene. In New Mexico, Reies López Tijerina formed the Alianza Federal de los Pueblos Libres (Federal Alliance of Free Peoples). Tijerina believed that Hispanic Americans in the state should have the lands returned to them that Anglos had taken away many years before.

5. José Angel Gutiérrez of Texas started a new political party, La Raza Unida. **La raza** is a Spanish term meaning "the race." It refers to all Spanish-speaking people in the Western Hemisphere. The word **Chicanos** was used at first by Mexican-American workers, not middle-class Mexican Americans, to refer to themselves. La Raza Unida gave Chicanos pride in themselves. It supported everything from community classes to draft counseling during the Vietnam War. Other leaders, such as María Hernández, who had been active against segregated schools in the 1930s, spoke at the party's rallies. In 1970, Gutiérrez and two other members of his La Raza Unita party won seats on the school board of Crystal City, Texas.

6. Beginning in 1970, courts began to rule that Hispanic Americans were an ethnic minority. That began to make it easier to win legal battles against discrimination. Hispanic Americans were making big strides.

▲ César Chávez (lower right) has been a national leader of the farm worker movement.

Understanding What You Have Read

A. In each of the sentences that follow, the underlined word or words make the sentence true or false. If the sentence is true, write **T** in the blank before it. If it is false, write the word or words that will make it true.

_____ 1. César Chávez started a national boycott against <u>tomatoes</u>.

_____ 2. The farm workers strike that began in 1965 lasted <u>five</u> years.

_____ 3. José Angel Gutiérrez was elected to the Crystal City <u>City Council</u>.

_____ 4. <u>Corky Gonzales</u> wanted lands returned to Hispanic New Mexicans.

B. Match each person in Column A with the organization he founded in Column B. Write the correct letter in each blank.

Column A	Column B
_____ 1. César Chávez	a. United Farm Workers Organizing Committee
_____ 2. José Angel Gutiérrez	b. Alianza Federal de los Pueblos Libres
_____ 3. Reies López Tijerina	c. La Raza Unida

Daily Life

Farm Workers' Flag. Throughout much of history, groups have made flags, banners, political buttons, or other objects that tell in a few words or pictures what their goals are. During the grape pickers' strike, the farm workers' union needed a symbol to show their strength. Manuel Chávez, César Chávez's cousin, designed this flag for the National Farm Workers Association (NFWA). The flag was first used at a meeting in Fresno, California, in 1962.

The Spanish word *Huelga* on the flag means "strike." Manuel Chávez explained that the black eagle was the symbol of the Aztecs, the Native American ancestors of many Chicanos. "When that eagle flies," said Manuel Chávez, "that's when the farm workers' problems are going to be solved."

1. Do you think that the eagle was a good choice for this flag? Why or why not? _____

_____

2. If you designed a flag to represent your school, what would it look like? Why?

_____

_____

Spotlight on People

Rodolfo "Corky" Gonzales. Rodolfo "Corky" Gonzales was a professional boxer. He is still fighting but not in a ring. Gonzales was born in a Denver barrio. Boxing was a way out of the poverty faced by his family of farm workers. He became a contender for the world featherweight title, but quit boxing to enter business. In the years ahead he would be a successful businessman, an insurance agent, a government official, a playwright, and a poet.

The job closest to Gonzales's heart was helping other Hispanic Americans. He served as a Democratic appointee under President Lyndon Johnson. However, party politics disappointed him. He felt there had to be a better way to help Hispanic Americans. In 1966, Gonzales founded La Cruzada Para La Justicia (The Crusade for Justice). Its purpose was to get Chicanos involved in politics and to improve their lives both socially and economically. Although there was no reason to believe this, some people felt that the Crusade for Justice was another Communist conspiracy.

Gonzales organized young people, led marches, and spoke out against discrimination. Unlike his fellow activist, César Chávez, Gonzales does not want Hispanic Americans to blend into American society. He feels they must form their own power base and take pride in their separateness. His speeches, plays, and poems celebrate Chicanos as a "bronze people with a bronze culture" going all the way back to the ancient **Aztecs,** Native Americans of Mexico. His famous poem "I am Joaquín" ends with the words, "I will ENDURE." Today, Gonzales continues to use his many talents to help Mexican Americans.

Recalling the Facts

Choose each correct answer and write the letter in the space provided.

_____ 1. Corky Gonzales became a boxer because he
   a. wanted to escape poverty.
   b. liked to beat up people.
   c. had no other abilities.

_____ 2. Corky Gonzales was never a
   a. businessman.
   b. poet.
   c. boxing coach.

_____ 3. The Aztecs were
   a. Mexican Native Americans.
   b. Spanish explorers.
   c. Chicano workers.

_____ 4. Corky Gonzales wants Chicanos to
   a. blend into society.
   b. return to Mexico.
   c. take pride in their separateness.

_____ 5. César Chávez and Corky Gonzales
   a. have the same plan for change.
   b. have different solutions to problems.
   c. are bitter enemies.

_____ 6. The purpose of the Crusade for Justice was to
   a. get Hispanic Americans back in school.
   b. involve Chicanos in politics.
   c. demonstrate for world peace.

Using Primary Sources

The Women's Movement. During the 1960s and early 1970s, many women began to demand more rights. They wanted equal pay for equal work, greater job opportunities for women, and government-funded day-care centers. Hispanic-American women formed organizations, such as La Comisión Femenil Mexicana in 1970, to seek women's rights. Women also worked for a greater say in groups such as La Raza Unida political party, to which both men and women belonged. Here are parts of the "Raza Women's Platform" of the Raza Unida political party.

> We shall respect the right of self-determination for . . . women to state what their . . . needs and problems are, and how they feel that these needs can be met and these problems can be eliminated, as a basic principle of our party.
>
> The party encourages La Raza women to meet in Raza women's groups . . . to discuss the . . . needs of Raza women they feel must be acted upon. We encourage that these groups . . . participate . . . politically . . . in all levels of the struggle.
>
> The party will include Raza women in all decision-making meetings, paying them due respect when they offer opinions and speak. . . .
>
> Raza men and women both will cooperate fully, in this party and at home, in . . . freeing . . . women . . . and in working actively towards the elimination [ending] of all attitudes and practices that have relegated [given a low place to] . . . women . . . to the [low] positions they are now in.
>
> Child-care centers controlled by Raza must be made available for Raza in schools, workplaces, and neighborhoods, totally free of charge. . . .

What are three of the goals this organization stated it would work for to improve the position of women? _____

_____

CHAPTER REVIEW: CRITICAL THINKING

You can **summarize** information, or write it in a short way, to help you remember it. Read each topic listed below. Then write a one-line headline about what you have read in this chapter.

1. Hispanic-American workers' organizations: _____

   _____

2. Hispanic-American political organizations: _____

   _____

3. Hispanic-American women's movement: _____

   _____

Chapter 10 CUBA AND THE DOMINICAN REPUBLIC

AIM: How did political change in Cuba result in new immigration to the United States? How did the United States deal with problems with Cuba and the Dominican Republic?

1. Why did many Cubans come to the United States in the 1960s? In 1934, the United States had decided that it would no longer interfere directly in Cuban affairs. However, from the 1930s to 1959, Cuba was controlled by Fulgencio Batista. For much of that time he ruled as a dictator. In 1959, Batista was overthrown by a revolution led by Fidel Castro. Many Cubans thought Castro would give them more freedom. Instead, he set up a Communist government that many Cubans did not approve of. Thousands of Cubans fled their homeland by boat and plane. Some went to Central and South America. Many more came to the United States. Thousands settled in Miami, Florida.

2. In 1962, the United States discovered that the Soviet Union was building missile bases in Cuba, only 90 miles from the United States. President Kennedy told the American people that the United States Navy and Air Force would stop any ship delivering arms to Cuba. The United States set up a **blockade** to keep the ships from reaching Cuba. Soviet ships bringing more weapons turned back, and the missiles built in Cuba were removed. The Cuban **missile crisis** ended all relations between the United States and Cuba for many years.

3. In 1965, Castro said that those Cubans who wanted to join their relatives in the United States would be allowed to go. The United States hired two planes to leave each day from near Havana with refugees. **Freedom Airlift,** as it was called, brought 4,000 Cubans to the United States each month for many years. They arrived here with little more than the clothes they wore. The Castro government took the homes and property of those who left. Once they arrived in the United States, the United States government helped them find homes and jobs. Many of these new arrivals moved to Miami, Florida.

4. The United States became directly involved in another Latin American country. Two years after Batista was overthrown in Cuba, another Latin-American dictator met his end. Rafael Trujillo Molina had controlled the Dominican Republic for 30 years. He was assassinated in 1961. Several people ruled after Trujillo. Then, in 1965, rebels captured parts of Santo Domingo, the capital. President Lyndon Johnson sent United States troops in to protect Americans, keep order, and prevent Communist rebels from taking over the country. Five Latin American countries also sent troops. An agreement was reached, and a new election was held. All American troops were off the island by September 1966.

▲ Freedom Airlift, 1965. Cuban political refugees arrive in the United States.

Understanding What You Have Read

Place the events below in the correct time order by writing the numbers 1 through 5 in the blanks.

_____ **a.** President Kennedy warns the Soviet Union to remove missiles from Cuba.

_____ **b.** Fidel Castro takes over Cuba.

_____ **c.** Relations between Cuba and the United States are cut off.

_____ **d.** The Freedom Airlift begins.

_____ **e.** Un   d States troops arrive in the Dominican Republic.

Building Geography Skills

By 1961, the Cuban exiles did not expect to stay long in the United States. They thought Castro would soon be overthrown. To bring about his downfall, the United States government supported about 1,500 mostly Cuban invaders in a secret invasion. At dawn on April 17, 1961, a fleet of ships approached the **Bay of Pigs** on Cuba's coast. Castro's army was ready. During the attempted invasion, some of the anti-Castro fighters were killed. The rest were taken prisoner. They remained in prison for nearly two years. They were finally released in exchange for food and medicine from the United States. It was clear Castro was securely in power and the **exiles** in Miami would not be going home soon.

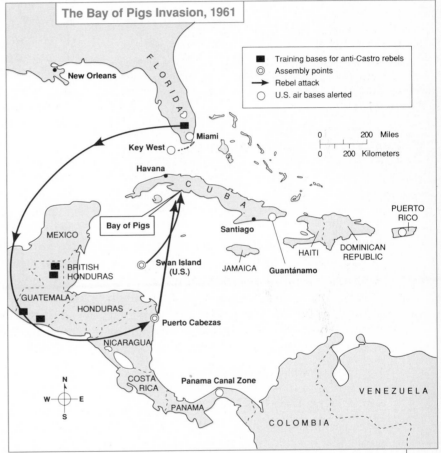

The Bay of Pigs Invasion, 1961

Legend:
- ■ Training bases for anti-Castro rebels
- ◎ Assembly points
- → Rebel attack
- ○ U.S. air bases alerted

Study the map. Then answer the following questions.

1. On which coast of Cuba is the Bay of Pigs located, the north, the south, the east, or the west? _____

2. What are two countries in which anti-Castro rebels were trained for the Bay of Pigs invasion? _____

3. What American-owned island was an assembly point for the anti-Castro rebels?
   _____

4. What was one of the United States air bases closest to the Bay of Pigs? _____

Armando Valladares. In 1960, a 23-year-old Cuban office worker was arrested for questioning the Communist government of Fidel Castro. The worker, Armando Valladares, spent 22 years in prison for "offenses against state authorities." As a political prisoner, or **plantado**, Valladares was treated worse than other prisoners. He was tortured and beaten constantly. Valladares spent months alone in a darkened cell and was fed only boiled oats. Prison authorities said he would be released if he would swear his loyalty to Castro. Time after time, Valladares refused.

· He found the strength to resist in religion and art. He became a Christian in prison and began writing poetry about his grim life behind bars. He also met Martha López, whose father was also a *plantado*. They fell in love, and in 1969 they were allowed to marry. The authorities believed that if Valladares had a wife, he would be more willing to give up his beliefs to win his freedom. Instead, Valladares had Martha move to Miami, where she would be safe. Martha had her husband's collected writings published in the United States. His poems were now read by people around the world. Amnesty International, a human rights group, spoke out for the release of Valladares as did many people in the United States.

Finally, in October 1982, Armando Valladares became a free man. Today, he lives in the United States with his wife. However, he has not forgotten his life as a prisoner. As a U.S. delegate to the UN Human Rights Commission, he continues to speak out against Castro's Cuba. He hopes that the hundreds of remaining *plantados* will someday follow him to freedom.

Recalling the Facts

Match each letter in Column A with the words that identify it in Column B. Write the correct letter in each blank.

Column A	Column B
_____ 1. Amnesty International	a. the year Valladares got married
_____ 2. *plantados*	b. the year Valladares was released from jail
_____ 3. 1960	c. Cuban political prisoners
_____ 4. UN Human Rights Commission	d. organization that called for Valladares's release from jail
_____ 5. 1982	e. the year Valladares went to prison
_____ 6. 1969	f. Valladares is a delegate of this group

The Arts and Technology

Poetry. This poem was written by Armando Valladares while he was in a Cuban prison. At one point he had no paper or pen. He wrote on a blank prescription form. He used a sliver of wood for a pen and Mercurochrome medicine for ink. He ended this message with the words, "My situation is difficult, but I feel and am a free man."

In 1980, Valladares was awarded the Freedom Prize for his prison poetry by the French chapter of P.E.N., an international writers' group. The story of his days in prison, *Against All Hope,* was published in the United States in 1986.

> I still have my smile
> for my pride in feeling a free man
> and in my soul a garden
> of small, undying flowers.
> They do not want me to write
> They took away the pens
> the pencils
> but I still have life's ink
> my own blood
> and with it I can write poems.

1. Although in prison, Valladares refers to himself as a "free man" in his poem. Why?

   _____

   _____

2. Instead of using the word *hope*, the poet describes the hope in his soul as if it were what? Why is this a good description? _____

   _____

3. Write a short poem describing your reaction to an event discussed in this book.

   _____

   _____

   _____

   _____

CHAPTER REVIEW: CRITICAL THINKING

Recognizing causes and effects can help you to understand history.

1. If the Bay of Pigs invasion had succeeded, how do you think it would have affected Cuban migration to the United States? _____

   _____

2. In 1965, United States troops landed in the Dominican Republic. What were the causes of this military action? _____

   _____

Chapter 11 PUERTO RICANS TODAY

AIM: What contributions have Puerto Ricans today made to the United States?

1. There are over 2.7 million Puerto Ricans on the United States mainland. Nearly half of them live in New York State. Many other Puerto Ricans live in cities in New Jersey, Illinois, Florida, and California. This number does not include the more than 3.3 million who live on the island of Puerto Rico.

2. The oldest Puerto Rican community in the United States is **El Barrio.** It is located in New York City. Here the people keep alive their language, culture, and traditions. They have started important places to preserve their culture. El Museo del Barrio is an art museum in New York that shows the works of Puerto Rican artists. The Puerto Rican Traveling The-atre is supported by the Puerto Rican actress Miriam Colón.

3. There are many groups that have formed to help Puerto Ricans in Puerto Rico and on the mainland. ASPIRA is Spanish for "to strive." This group encourages young Puerto Ricans to get a better education. It also provides scholarships to help them go to college. In Puerto Rico today, over 40 percent of all Puerto Ricans between the ages of 18 and 24 are in college. The Institute of Puerto Rican Culture gives an annual Puerto Rican Theater Festival. It also gives scholarships to young Puerto Rican artists to study in Europe.

4. Puerto Ricans have contributed to the United States in politics and government. One important example is Teodoro Moscoso, who became the first Puerto Rican representing the United States as an ambassador. In 1970, Herman Badillo became the first Puerto Rican elected to the United States House of Representatives. From 1946 to 1969, Felisa Rincón de Gautier was mayor of San Juan, the capital of Puerto Rico. As mayor, she opened the doors of city hall to the citizens of San Juan. She listened to their problems, and she solved them. She became so well known for her work that she was named one of the 100 outstanding women in the world.

5. Puerto Ricans have made important contributions as doctors, lawyers, and teachers, as well as in sports and the arts. Roberto Clemente and Orlando Cepeda have become baseball legends in the United States. Cindy Colberg and Grace Valdez have both won silver medals representing Puerto Rico in the Central American Games tennis competition. In the arts, Chita Rivera and José Ferrer have brought entertainment to millions of American television and movie viewers. People who love classical music enjoy Jesús María Sanromá's skill on the piano.

6. These are just a few of the many Puerto Ricans who have become positive role models for thousands of young people. Puerto Ricans will continue to play a vital role.

▲ Felisa Rincón de Gautier was mayor of San Juan, Puerto Rico, from 1946 to 1969.

A. Match each word or words in Column A with the definition in Column B. Write the correct letter in each blank.

Column A

_____ 1. Puerto Rican Traveling Theatre

_____ 2. El Barrio

_____ 3. ASPIRA

_____ 4. commonwealth

_____ 5. Institute of Puerto Rican Culture

_____ 6. El Museo del Barrio

Column B

a. organization helping Puerto Ricans through education

b. exhibits Puerto Rican art

c. sponsors Puerto Rican Theater Festival

d. New York City acting company

e. oldest Puerto Rican community in New York

f. status of Puerto Rico in relation to the United States

B. In each of the sentences that follow, the underlined word makes the sentence true or false. If the sentence is true, write **T** in the blank before it. If it is false, write the word or words in the blank that will make it true.

_____ 1. Between the United States and the Puerto Rico there are about <u>5.8</u> million Puerto Ricans.

_____ 2. Felisa Rincón de Gautier was mayor of San Juan for <u>two</u> years.

_____ 3. Almost half of all Puerto Ricans in the United States live in <u>Los Angeles</u>.

_____ 4. Orlando Cepeda is a <u>baseball</u> legend in the United States.

Building Geography Skills

Study the map. Then answer the questions.

1. If you flew in a straight line from San Juan, Puerto Rico, to New York City, what direction would your plane fly—northeast, southwest, or northwest?

   _____

2. According to the map, in which cities on the mainland do many Puerto Ricans live?

   _____

   _____

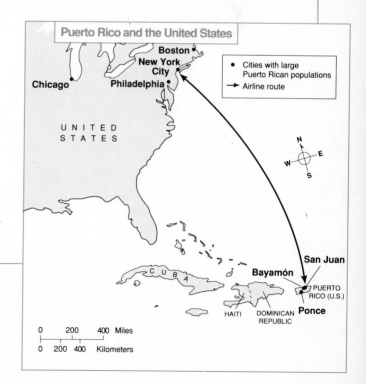

Spotlight on People

Rita Moreno. On December 11, 1931, Rita Moreno was born in Humacao, a small Puerto Rican city. Her birth name was Rosa Dolores Alverio. As a very young girl, she and her mother moved from Puerto Rico to New York City. When she entered school, she fell behind, because she had difficulty speaking in English. Her greatest enjoyment came from the dance classes that she had after school.

From her teenage years to her mid-twenties, Moreno had a series of dancing and acting jobs. As a teenager, she started singing and doing flamenco dances in clubs to help the family income. Moreno got her start in Hollywood dubbing voices for the Spanish translations of American movies. In 1950 she made her first movie. It was a reform school drama titled *So Young, So Bad*. Her Hollywood name became Rosita Moreno. Later Rosita was shortened to Rita.

For a while, Moreno was not happy with her acting roles. In 1961, her luck changed. She played the role of Anita in the movie *West Side Story*. The movie told the story of tragic love between a Puerto Rican girl and an Italian boy in New York City. The movie won a total of ten Oscar awards. Moreno won the Oscar for best supporting actress.

Moreno went on to win three more important awards. In 1972, she and her television co-stars won a Grammy Award for *The Electric Company*'s record album. The show taught reading in a fun way. In 1975, Moreno won a Tony for best supporting actress in the Broadway play *The Ritz*. And in 1977, she won a Emmy Award for her guest appearance on television's *The Muppet Show*. Today Rita Moreno divides her time between her family and her successful career.

Recalling the Facts

1. Before coming to New York City, Rita Moreno's home was in _____.

2. As a young girl, Moreno's lessons in _____ were her first step toward her career as a performer.

3. Moreno won an Oscar award for her role as Anita in _____.

4. Moreno's television Grammy Award was for _____.

5. For Moreno's role in the play *The Ritz*, she won a _____.

6. In 1977 Moreno won an Emmy Award for _____.

48

The Arts and Technology

Popular Music. José Feliciano's music is a special blend of soul, folk, Latin, and blues styles. In 1968, his soulful version of the Doors's song "Light My Fire" was his big break. It became a number-one song on the pop charts. Feliciano won two Grammy awards for that song. One of the awards was for Best New Artist. The other was for Best Contemporary Pop Vocal Male Performer.

▲ José Feliciano, a great vocal performer, has been blind since birth.

1. Upon whom are singers, such as José Feliciano, usually dependent for their success?

   _____

   _____

2. How might Feliciano's blindness help or hinder his music career? _____

   _____

   _____

CHAPTER REVIEW: CRITICAL THINKING

Puerto Rico has an unusual status. It is part of the United States, yet separate. Some people think Puerto Rico should become the 51st state of the United States. Others want Puerto Rico to remain a commonwealth. Others feel it should become an independent country.

1. Do you think Puerto Rico should become a U.S. state or a separate country or remain a commonwealth? Which do you think would be better for the people of Puerto Rico?

   _____

   _____

2. If you were Puerto Rican, would you rather live on the mainland or in Puerto Rico? Give

   some reasons for your answer. _____

   _____

Chapter 12 MEXICAN AMERICANS TODAY

AIM: Who are Mexican Americans today? How are they preserving their culture?

1. Mexican Americans have always been and still are the largest group of Hispanic-Americans in the United States. By 1990, there will probably be about 17 million Mexican Americans. Almost three-fourths of those Mexican Americans live in the Southwest and Pacific states regions.

2. Today, most Mexican Americans live in cities such as Los Angeles, San Antonio, Santa Fe, and El Paso. Los Angeles has the largest Mexican-American population of any city in the United States. The heritage of Spain and Mexico is seen in the architecture of these cities. For example, there is a section of Los Angeles called the Pueblo de Los Ángeles. This area has been restored to look like a village of Old Mexico. It is on the spot where Mexican settlers founded Los Angeles almost 200 years ago.

3. Mexican Americans are proud of their Mexican heritage. They are also proud to be American citizens. Like other ethnic groups, they make a special effort to preserve their own culture. Mexican Americans preserve their language by speaking Spanish in the home and in their neighborhoods. In San Antonio, there is a Mexican American Cultural Exchange Institute. It was formed to share and preserve the customs and language of Mexico.

4. There are many groups that have formed to help Mexican Americans. La Raza Unida (People Together) was founded in 1970 by José Angel Gutiérrez. La Raza Unida is a political party that nominates Mexican Americans to run for public office. The Southwest Voter Registration Education Project (SVREP) doubled Mexican-American voter registration from 1976 to 1985.

5. Mexican Americans have contributed to the United States by taking leadership roles. In 1981, Henry Cisneros became the first Mexican-American mayor of San Antonio in 140 years. He has brought new businesses and jobs to the city. In 1982, Gloria Molina became the first Mexican-American woman elected to the California State Assembly. Throughout her career, she has been active in community concerns in Los Angeles.

6. Emilie Cacho is one example among many Mexican Americans who work hard to fulfill their dreams. Cacho's parents were immigrant farm workers. They believed in education, and Cacho graduated from the University of California. She has been a social worker and a teacher. Today she is a counselor especially for Mexican Americans.

7. Mexican Americans have proven throughout their history that they can solve problems through positive action. Mexican Americans will continue to play a vital role in the growth of the United States.

▲ Henry Cisneros is mayor of San Antonio, Texas.

Understanding What You Have Read

Write your answers to the following questions in the spaces provided.

1. In what regions do most Mexican Americans live? _____

2. What is the Pueblo de Los Ángeles? _____

3. In what ways do Mexican Americans preserve their culture? _____

4. What are the firsts represented in Cisneros and Molina?_____

5. Why was education important for Emilie Cacho? _____

Building Geography Skills

Study the map. Then answer the questions.

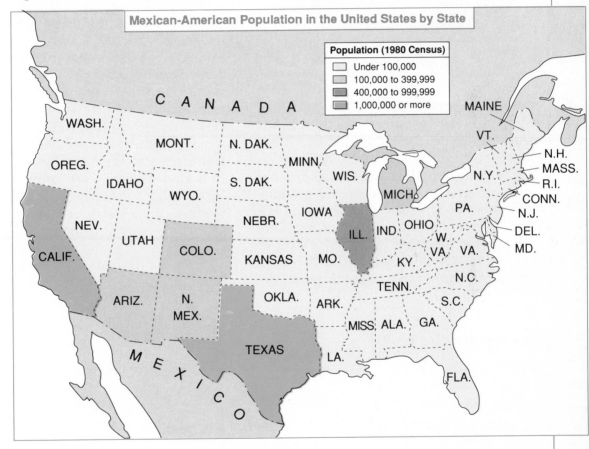

1. How many states have fewer than 100,000 Mexican Americans? _____

2. Which states have one million or more Mexican Americans? _____

_____

3. Which state is in the same Mexican-American population range as Colorado, New Mexico, and Arizona? _____

4. What is the Mexican-American population range of Illinois? _____

Spotlight on People

Gloria Moreno-Wycoff. If you asked Gloria Moreno-Wycoff what her gold mine is, she would tell you the public library. When Moreno-Wycoff was a child, her mother stressed the importance of education to her and her brother and sister. At Moreno-Wycoff's high school in Los Angeles in 1949, she was the keynote speaker for her class. After being a mother of five, she went to college. In 1984, she graduated with honors and a master of public administration degree at the University of Southern California.

Moreno-Wycoff was introduced to local politics in 1962. She worked to help her brother in his first successful political campaign. From that experience, she realized that Mexican-American women did not have enough voice or involvement in community politics and activities.

In response to this need, Moreno-Wycoff became the founding president of Femenil de Rio Hondo. It is a Hispanic-American women's organization that works to improve the image of Mexican-American women. In 1980, Moreno-Wycoff became the president of La Comisión Femenil Mexicana Nacional. She has represented Hispanic-American women in a meeting with former President Jimmy Carter in Washington, D.C.

Moreno-Wycoff considers her greatest accomplishment has been to help troubled teenagers and their families. Through La Comisión Femenil, she established Casa Victoria. It is a group home to help troubled teenage girls who are on probation. Moreno-Wycoff also feels a great deal of satisfaction in helping teens get away from substance abuse and back into the gold mine found in books.

Recalling the Facts

1. Moreno-Wycoff thought the public library was a gold mine because _____

   _____

2. Moreno-Wycoff graduated with a master of _____
   in 1984.

3. Moreno-Wycoff became concerned that _____
   did not have enough influence in the community.

4. Moreno-Wycoff founded a women's group called _____.

5. La Comisión Femenil Mexicana Nacional works to improve the image of _____.

6. Today Moreno-Wycoff contributes significantly to helping _____

   _____.

The Arts and Technology

▲ Linda Ronstadt sings songs reflecting her Mexican heritage.

To my father with affection . . .

Those long summer evenings of my childhood, when the moon made strange patterns on Father's guitar as he sang enchanting songs to me, are no more. But the imagination hears the romance and wistfulness of their melodies, hears them with a sweetness as subtle as the fragrance of wildflowers dried in herbs.

—Luisa Ronstadt, 1946

Canciones. The words above appear on the cover of Linda Ronstadt's album *Canciones de Mi Padre.* They were written by Ronstadt's aunt. They originally introduced a book of collected songs from the hometown of Ronstadt's grandfather—Sonora, Mexico.

Many of the songs were sung to Ronstadt by her father when she was a child in Tucson, Arizona. They include Mexican cowboy songs called **rancheras** and **huapangos**.

1. What, do you think, is the meaning of Luisa Ronstadt's words on Linda Ronstadt's album cover? _____

_____

2. How do you think this album contributes to preserving the heritage of Mexican Americans? _____

_____

CHAPTER REVIEW: CRITICAL THINKING ▮▮▮▮

1. Why is participation in government one of the best ways for Mexican Americans to bring about change?_____

_____

2. Why is it important to understand your own culture *and* the culture of other ethnic groups?

_____

_____

Chapter 13 CUBAN AMERICANS TODAY

AIM: What has motivated recent Cuban-American immigrants to achieve so much in the short time they have been in the United States?

1. Nowhere is the spirit of Cuban Americans more alive than in the city of Miami, Florida. So many Cubans now live in this city that some people call it "North Cuba." "Little Havana," the most concentrated Cuban part of Miami, is filled with Cuban-run businesses and stores. Cuban Americans own banks, major corporations, and businesses. Four Cuban-American women, Maria Elena Toraño, Teresa Zubizarreta, Aida Levitán, and Ana María Haar, own large public relations firms. Cuban Americans are the heads of several universities. Cuban culture can be seen throughout the city and the country For example, Fernando Bujones is one of the top figures in the world of ballet.

2. Why have Cubans done so well here? They were mostly motivated by the problems they had to overcome just to get here. They had to give up their homeland and possessions and put up with the Castro government. Like European immigrants before them, they came here with nothing but were determined to become somebody. For example, one refugee, Carlos Arboleya, arrived in the United States with $40 in his pocket. Today, he is the vice chairman of a major Florida bank.

3. Another reason for their success is the Cuban tradition of helping each other. The earliest refugees were mostly wealthy people, professionals, and businesspeople. Once established, they gave jobs and other aid to the poorer Cubans who came after them. In addition, more Cuban-American women than Anglo women work outside the home. That has helped to make Cuban-American households better off financially. The three-generation household has also helped to maintain language and cultural values and behaviors.

4. Cuban immigration to the United States did not end with the Freedom Airlift in the 1970s. In 1980, Fidel Castro released 125,000 refugees, some of whom were in Cuban prisons. The **Mariel boat people,** as they were called, were not as welcome in the United States as earlier refugees. Since some had criminal records, Americans feared them. However, most of them have fitted in well.

5. There are many important Cuban-American organizations. Among them are the Latin Builders Association and CAMACOL (the Latin Chamber of Commerce). However, none is more influential than the Cuban American National Foundation. Its president, Jorge Más Canosa, has made it into a very powerful political group. **Radio Martí,** whose broadcasts reach Cuba, has been its crowning achievement.

6. Not all Cuban Americans live in Florida. Over a quarter of them live in New Jersey, New York, and California. The largest concentration of Cuban Americans, outside of Miami, is in West New York and Union City, New Jersey. The avenue between the two cities is full of Cuban-owned shops and stores.

7. Today there are about one million Cuban Americans. Although they are a small part of the total Hispanic-American population, they are the most successful. Nearly 30 percent of them earn $25,000 a year or more.

▲ Many Cuban Americans are business people who own their own shops and companies.

Understanding What You Have Read

A. Write the correct word from the list in the blank to complete each sentence.

1970	businesses	Miami	small
Union City	large	1980	airplanes

1. "Little Havana" is located in _____ .

2. The **Mariel boat people** came to the U.S. in _____ .

3. Cuban Americans make up a _____ part of the total Hispanic-American population.

4. Many Cuban Americans own their own _____ .

B. In each of the sentences that follow, the underlined word or words make the sentence true or false. If the sentence is true, write **T** in the blank before it. If it is false, write the word or words that will make it true.

_____ 1. There is a high concentration of Cubans in <u>New York</u>.

_____ 2. Cuban Americans are generally <u>younger</u> than other Hispanic Americans.

_____ 3. There are about <u>one million</u> Cuban Americans in the United States.

_____ 4. Close to a third of all Cuban Americans earn <u>$50,000</u> a year or more.

Building Graph Skills

The bar graph below shows the percentages of Cuban Americans in different jobs. Study the graph and then answer the questions.

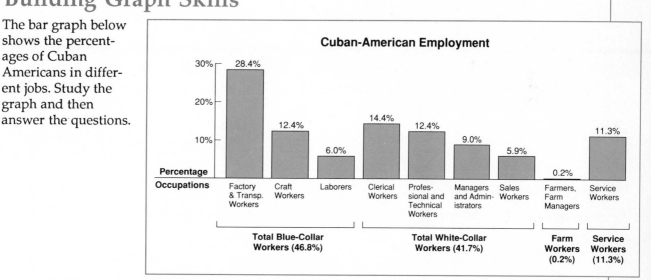

1. Where are the fewest Cuban Americans employed? _____

2. What percentage of Cuban Americans are service workers? _____

3. What kinds of **white-collar** and **blue-collar** work employ the same number of Cuban

   Americans? _____

   _____

Spotlight on People

▲ Xavier Suarez and his wife, Rita Suarez, worked together during his campaign.

Xavier Suarez. "With the poor people of this earth, I want to share my fate."

These stirring words were written by Cuban poet and patriot José Martí. They were spoken by Xavier Suarez as he was sworn in as the first Cuban-American mayor of Miami, Florida, in 1985.

The young mayor has tried to live these words. He has helped find jobs for unemployed Black youths. He has made the city streets safer for citizens by putting more police where they can be seen. Suarez has worked to make Miami a city for all its people—Hispanics, Blacks, and Anglos.

Suarez is the ninth of fourteen children. He came from a middle-class Cuban family. When Castro came to power, his father and sisters were put into jail. The Suarezes soon fled to the United States, where young Xavier learned English in only two months.

Suarez graduated from Villanova University and earned a law degree from Harvard. His first attempts at politics were not successful. He lost in two elections for the Miami City Commission. Despite these losses, he ran for mayor against the popular six-term mayor, Puerto Rican Maurice Ferre. Suarez won. Suarez has a bright political future.

Recalling the Facts

Match each person or place in Column A with the words that identify it in Column B. Write the correct letter in each blank.

Column A	Column B
_____ 1. Xavier Suarez	**a.** former Puerto Rican mayor of Miami
_____ 2. Harvard University	**b.** Cuban leader who arrested Suarez's father
_____ 3. José Martí	**c.** college Suarez graduated from
_____ 4. Fidel Castro	**d.** where Suarez earned his law degree
_____ 5. Villanova University	**e.** first Cuban-American mayor of Miami
_____ 6. Maurice Ferre	**f.** famous Cuban poet

The Arts and Technology

◀ Cuban-American artist Demi's paintings often show children in dreamlike situations, such as this one entitled *Girl Playing with Masks*.

Painting. The artist Demi is one of many Cubans who came to the United States. In 1962, when Demi was six years old, her father was executed as a political prisoner. Demi's family left Cuba to search for freedom.

Demi has grown up in the United States. She is a United States citizen. Like many other Cuban-American artists, she lives and paints near Miami, Florida. Her paintings are well-known today.

Although Demi has spent most of her life in freedom in the United States, her paintings reach back to her childhood. She has never forgotten the execution of her father in Cuba. Her style of painting is, in a way, childlike. Simple, innocent children appear with simple objects. Those objects, however, hold both beauty and danger.

Demi said, "My paintings blossom from the inner depth of those childhood memories. My work grows out of the positive belief that if I expose injustices they eventually will be corrected."

1. This painting is called _____. The child looks sweet and innocent. How does the rest of the painting make you feel? What details in the painting add to your feeling? _____

2. Do you find Demi's art to be optimistic or pessimistic? Why? _____

_____

CHAPTER REVIEW: CRITICAL THINKING

A **hypothesis** is a guess that you make because it seems likely to be true. When you make a hypothesis, you try to find evidence to support it.

1. Why do so many Cuban Americans live in the Miami area of Florida? Support your answer.

_____

2. In general, Cuban Americans are more politically conservative than other Hispanic Americans. Why do you think this is so? _____

_____

14 OTHER HISPANICS TODAY

AIM: Who are the other Hispanic Americans? Why did they choose to come to the United States?

1. No category of Hispanic Americans is made up of so many different groups as the one sometime called "other Hispanics." This category includes Hispanics from Caribbean islands, from Central and South America, and from Spain. Among "other Hispanics" are people who are only part Hispanic and those who have parents of different Hispanic groups. Some have been in the United States for generations. Most are newly arrived immigrants or children of immigrants.

2. What have been other Hispanics' reasons for coming to the United States? Some came because the economy in their country could not use their highly special skills. A high percentage of them are highly skilled professionals—engineers, lawyers, architects. Others came because war, political changes, or revolution drove them from their homelands. This has been true in such different countries as Argentina and El Salvador. About one out of 10 Nicaraguans—over 250,000 people—have left their Marxist-controlled country for the United States since 1979. One young Nicaraguan described his reasons this way. "My life became too complicated. I could not live in peace." Like Cuban immigrants, political refugees from these countries wanted freedom, democracy, and political safety.

3. Still other immigrants came to avoid the low or falling wages and the high food prices that made it difficult for their families to survive. Many immigrants, especially from Central America, came here looking for any work they could find. These are mostly poor farmers and townspeople from countries such as Guatemala. A middle-aged Guatemalan listed her reason for leaving: "the poverty, the government corruption [dishonesty], and the political persecution [attacks]. Unlike many of the other Latin-American immigrants, most have very little education and find work in low-paying jobs in service industries and factories.

4. Part Hispanics have one parent who is Hispanic. This parent is often a well-educated South American or a Hispanic who has lived in the United States for a long time. Mixed Hispanics have parents of two different Hispanic groups. They are at every economic level. Mixed Hispanics most often live in large cities where people from different Hispanic American backgrounds meet at work or at social events.

5. There are about 4,200,000 "other Hispanics" in the United States today. Most of the 350,000 people from the Dominican Republic live in New York City. Colombians and people from Ecuador are also large groups, mainly in the Northeast. Nicaraguans have settled mainly in southeastern California. People from El Salvador moved to California and the Southwest.

6. Since "other Hispanics" belong to so many different groups, it is hard to generalize about them. "Other Hispanics" are often among the best-educated of all the Hispanic-American groups. Many of them are white-collar workers. Taken together, "other Hispanics" have a higher family income than do Puerto Ricans or Mexican Americans. "Other Hispanics" have fewer children and more elderly people among them. As is true of the rest of the Hispanic-American community, "other Hispanics" are proudly preserving much of their cultures, language, and traditions.

▲ Costa Rican dancers in traditional costumes take part in the United Hispanic-American parade in New York City.

Understanding What You Have Read

Write your answers to the following questions in the spaces provided.

1. List three of the reasons why "other Hispanics" have come to the United States.

   a. _____

   b. _____

   c. _____

2. List five countries from which "other Hispanics" have come to the United States.

   _____

   _____

++

Using Graph Skills

Study the circle graph. Then read the statements below. The underlined word or words make the statement true or false. If the statement is true, write **T** in the blank before it. If it is false, write the word or words that would make it true.

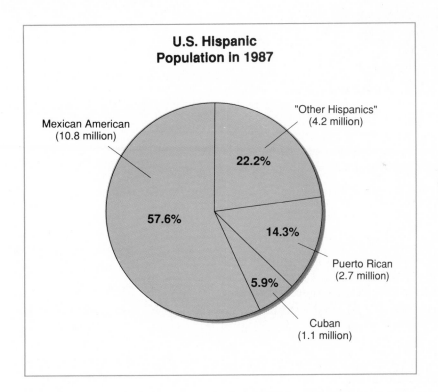

U.S. Hispanic Population in 1987

Mexican American (10.8 million) — 57.6%

"Other Hispanics" (4.2 million) — 22.2%

Puerto Rican (2.7 million) — 14.3%

Cuban (1.1 million) — 5.9%

_____ 1. In 1987 there were over <u>4 million</u> "other Hispanics" in the United States.

_____ 2. <u>Mainland Puerto Ricans</u> outnumber "other Hispanics" in the United States.

_____ 3. "Other Hispanics" are the <u>second largest</u> Hispanic group in the United States.

Raquel Welch. Raquel Welch is a famous movie star, but few people realize she is part Hispanic. Her real name is Raquel Tejada and her father was born in Bolivia. Her mother is English.

Raquel Tejada was born in 1940 in Chicago and grew up in California, where she took ballet lessons as a girl. She won her first beauty contest at age 14. She married her high school sweetheart, James Welch, at 18, but the couple separated three years later. Raquel Welch started taking acting classes at San Diego State College, did a little performing, and then moved to Dallas, Texas. There she worked as a waitress and model before making the big move to Hollywood to pursue a film career.

At first, she got only a few bit parts in movies. Then she met press agent Patrick Curtis and her luck changed. Curtis managed her career and got her a contract with Twentieth Century-Fox Studios. Within a short time, Raquel was an international star. The amazing part was, she had not yet appeared in one major movie.

Raquel Welch was known for years for her good looks and not her acting. However, she proved she was more than just a beauty queen. She played a roller derby player in *Kansas City Bomber* and an innocent heroine in *The Three Musketeers*. More recently, she became a Broadway star when she sang and danced in the hit stage musical *Woman of the Year*.

Recalling the Facts

Choose each correct answer and write the letter in the space provided.

_____ 1. Raquel Welch was born in
  a. Chicago.
  b. Bolivia.
  c. the Dominican Republic.

_____ 2. Raquel Welch changed her name from Tejada to Welch because
  a. Welch is an Anglo-sounding name.
  b. Welch was the name of her husband.
  c. she preferred a shorter name.

_____ 3. To prepare for her acting career, Raquel Welch
  a. took acting classes at a college.
  a. did not practice by performing in plays.
  c. studied in Hollywood.

_____ 4. Raquel Welch is
  a. not really Hispanic.
  b. mixed Hispanic.
  c. part Hispanic.

_____ 5. Raquel Welch became an international film star
  a. before she was in a major movie.
  b. after she was in a major movie.
  c. after she starred in a Broadway play.

The Arts and Technology

Ballet. World-famous ballerina Lupe Serrano has been called "one of the most brilliant technicians [experts at dance movement] of her generation." Serrano was born in Santiago, Chile. As a child, Serrano studied in Mexico City, where she had her first major performance at the age of 13. From 1953 to the early 1970s, she performed as a member of the American Ballet Theatre. She now teaches in Pennsylvania.

▲ Ballerina Lupe Serrano gave performances in major cities throughout the world.

1. In what **country did** Serrano give her first major performance? _____

2. The Hispanic influence on ballet has been enormous. Hispanic Americans head and perform in many of the country's regional ballet companies. Others are set designers, choreographers (those who arrange and compose the dances for ballets), and teachers. Still others are world-famous dancers. Write a brief letter to a regional ballet company in your state, or to the American Ballet Theatre or the New York City Ballet asking for information and brochures about their dancers. Then make a bulletin-board display.

CHAPTER SUMMARY: CRITICAL THINKING

1. What is the most important reason why "other Hispanics" want to come to the United States? Support your opinion. _____

   _____

2. What recent events in Central America might result in more Hispanics coming to the United States? _____

   _____

UNIT 3 REVIEW

Summary of the Unit

A few of the most important events and facts presented in Unit 3 are listed below. Write these in your notebook and add four others.

1. Hispanic Americans fought bravely in Korea and Vietnam, but they often returned home to find themselves ignored and unappreciated.
2. In the 1960s, Hispanic Americans developed strong unions for workers and discovered a new identity for themselves based on their past.
3. The rise of a Communist government in Cuba brought many thousands of Cuban political refugees to the United States in the 1960s and 1970s.
4. Puerto Ricans are United States citizens, whether they live in Puerto Rico or in the United States mainland.
5. Mexican Americans are the largest group of Hispanic Americans with the longest history here.
6. Cuban Americans have achieved much in the United States partly because of hardships they have endured in getting here.
7. Other Hispanic Americans include many different immigrant groups from the Caribbean, Central and South America, and Spain, as well as people who are mixed or part Hispanic.

Understanding What You Have Read

In each of the sentences that follow, the underlined word or words make the sentence true or false. If the sentence is true, write **T** in the blank before it. If it is false, write the word or words that will make it true.

_____ 1. The United States sent troops to the <u>Dominican Republic</u> in 1965.

_____ 2. A major farm workers' strike in California was led by <u>Reies López Tijerina</u>.

_____ 3. <u>Freedom Airlift</u> brought thousands of political refugees to the United States from Communist Cuba.

_____ 4. <u>Other Hispanics</u> are born American citizens.

_____ 5. Henry Cisneros and Xavier Suarez are leading Hispanic-American <u>governors</u>.

_____ 6. The state with the highest number of Cuban Americans is <u>Florida</u>.

Building Your Vocabulary

Select two of the following words, and write a sentence using each of them.

Chicanos   plantado   rancheras

1. _____

   _____

2. _____

   _____

Building Your Vocabulary (contd.)

Match each word or words in Column A with the correct meaning in Column B. Write the letter in each blank.

Column A

_____ 1. *aspira*

_____ 2. casualties

_____ 3. professionals

_____ 4. La Raza Unida

_____ 5. exile

_____ 6. boycott

_____ 7. dictator

_____ 8. Viet Cong

Column B

a. a political party that nominated Mexican Americans for public office

b. absolute ruler

c. to strive

d. Communist rebels in South Vietnam

e. the number wounded or killed in war

f. forced removal from one's country

g. refusal to buy something

h. highly skilled specialists such as lawyers and architects

Developing Ideas and Skills—Using a Time Line

Study the time line. Then answer the questions by writing the letter for the correct period of time in the space provided.

1952	1960	1968	1976	1984
A	B	C	D	

_____ 1. The Freedom Airlift from Cuba takes place.

_____ 2. César Chávez starts a national farm workers' organization.

_____ 3. Herman Badillo becomes the first Puerto Rican elected to the U.S. House of Representatives.

_____ 4. Large-scale immigration from Nicaragua begins.

Making History Live

1. Take part in a classroom debate over which is a more effective way to improve Hispanic Americans' lives—radical activism or the traditional political process. Use information from the unit and from library research to support your argument.

2. Write a report about one aspect of Puerto Rican life in New York City, Cuban-American life in Miami, or Mexican-American life in Los Angeles or another city in the Southwest. Research your report at your school library or public library.

3. Select one of the following Hispanic Americans. Either write a brief biography of that person or make a drawing or painting showing an important point in that person's life: Fernando Bujones, Vikki Carr, Roberto Clemente, José Ferrer, María Hernández, Lupe Serrano.

Chapter 15 BUSINESS AND LABOR

AIM: What businesses are owned by Hispanic Americans and how successful are they?

1. Hispanic Americans are an important part of the United States business community. They are skilled workers, managers, and owners. Hundreds of corporations and thousands of small businesses are owned, managed, and staffed by Hispanic Americans. Total sales for the top 500 Hispanic-owned corporations in 1986 was nearly $10 billion. They employed over 75,000 people, many of them Hispanic Americans. Not surprisingly most of these corporations are in the states with a high Hispanic population. These states include California, Florida, Texas, and New York.

2. Some corporations began to sell goods to Hispanic Americans. Goya Foods began as a neighborhood grocery store in New York City. The owners, Spanish immigrants, sold imported olive oil and sardines to their Hispanic customers. Today Goya is the fourth largest Hispanic-owned business in the United States. Bacardi Imports was founded in Santiago, Cuba, in 1862. Now Cuban-born Luis J. Echarte runs this largest of all Hispanic-American firms from its headquarters in Miami.

3. Hispanic-American women are also making their mark in business. About four out of every ten Hispanic-American households has at least one woman working full time outside the home. Mexican American Betty Rivera runs a huge car dealership in New Mexico. Ramona Acosta Bañuelos, former treasurer of the United States, heads Ramona's Mexican Food Products of Gardena, California, with sales in the millions of dollars. Puerto Rican Elda López-Rosich Himelbláu runs the San Juan Coal Company from her home in Matawan, New Jersey. Cuban American Teresa Zubizarreta runs a multi-million dollar ad agency in Miami. To help women in business, Dr. Sylvia Castillo founded the National Network of Hispanic Women. Women have also organized MANO (the Mexican American Business and Professional Association).

4. Hispanic businesses in many cities are booming. There are nearly 20,000 successful Cuban-American businesses in the Miami area, including supermarkets, drugstores, cigar factories, and banks. Chicago, San Antonio, and Los Angeles have a great variety of Hispanic-American businesses both large and small. New York City has hundreds of small restaurants and hundreds of neighborhood grocery stores called **bodegas.**

5. Seventy-five years ago, most Hispanic Americans were farm migrant workers. Today only 9 percent of them work on farms. About half of all Hispanic Americans are blue-collar workers. They drive trucks, operate machines, and are artisans. About 35 percent are white-collar workers. They are salespersons, clerks, managers, and professional people. Another 16 percent are involved in the service industries. They work in restaurants, hotels, and other places of business. Hispanic Americans continue to contribute to the business of the United States on every level.

▲ Part of Miami's business district is called Little Havana.

Understanding What You Have Read

Choose each correct answer and write the letter in the space provided.

_____ 1. Most of the largest Hispanic-owned corporations are in
    a. Massachusetts, Pennsylvania, Maryland, and Virginia.
    b. California, Florida, Texas, and New York.
    c. Washington, Oregon, Montana, and Wyoming.

_____ 2. The main idea of *paragraph 5* is that Hispanic Americans are
    a. among the chief executives of non-Hispanic businesses.
    b. not hired for top positions in any big corporations.
    c. mainly workers in small businesses.

_____ 3. The top 500 Hispanic-owned corporations had total sales in the late 1980s of about
    a. $5 million.   b. $10 billion.   c. $100 billion.

_____ 4. The number of Hispanic-American farm workers has decreased to fewer than
    a. one in 10 workers.   b. one in 20 workers.   c. one in 30 workers.

_____ 5. The largest group in the Hispanic-American work force is made up of
    a. farm workers.
    b. blue-collar workers, such as machine operators, factory workers, and truck drivers.
    c. white-collar workers, such as salespersons, clerks, managers, and professional people.

_____ 6. Hispanic-American women who are full-time workers outside the home can be found in
    a. one out of 10 Hispanic-American households.
    b. four out of 10 Hispanic-American households.
    c. six out of 10 Hispanic-American households.

Using Chart Skills

Read the chart. Then answer the questions.

1. What three kinds of businesses account for over half of the top Hispanic-owned corporations?

_____

_____

2. How many more Hispanic-owned retail businesses are there than finance corporations among the top 500? _____

3. Which business numbers one less than agriculture and other business? _____

_____

500 Largest Hispanic-owned Corporations in the United States	
Service businesses	105
Manufacturing	93
Wholesale businesses	82
Construction	73
Retail businesses	57
Food	34
Finance	27
Transportation	14
Agriculture and other businesses	15

Spotlight on People

Hector Barreto. When Hector Barreto first came to the United States, he expected to find a land with a "river of beans" and "trees of tortillas." This is what his friends back in Mexico told him America was like. He quickly learned otherwise. Barreto settled in Kansas City, Missouri. His first job was digging potatoes. He later got a job in a meat packing house.

The young Mexican would bring tacos for lunch. Everyone he worked with liked to try the tacos. So Hector borrowed money from relatives and opened a small restaurant. It was across the street from the meat packing house. Business was so good that he was able to open a second restaurant. Soon, he had saved enough money to go into the import and construction business.

Barreto wanted to share his success with other Hispanic Americans. He felt to improve their lives, they had to join together both politically and economically. In 1979, he founded the United States Hispanic Chamber of Commerce (USHCC) for Hispanic-American businesspeople. As president of USHCC, he met with President Reagan to discuss greater representation for Hispanic Americans in government and business. When Abel Quintel became president of USHCC in 1987, Barreto became chairman emeritus (retired) of the organization. What advice does Barreto have for young Hispanic Americans who want to succeed? "You can make it, if you apply yourself—if you sacrifice," he says. "There's light at the end of the tunnel. There are dreams you can fulfill."

Recalling the Facts

Choose each correct answer and write the letter in the space provided.

_____ 1. When Hector Barreto arrived in the United States he expected
    a. a hard life.
    b. to make a million dollars.
    c. a river of beans.

_____ 2. Barreto's first job was
    a. digging potatoes.
    b. working in a restaurant.
    c. hauling beef.
    d. picking grapes.

_____ 3. Barreto opened a restaurant with the help of
    a. the government.
    b. his relatives.
    c. his friends.
    d. his coworkers.

_____ 4. He founded the USHCC in
    a. 1975.
    b. 1977.
    c. 1979.
    d. 1985.

_____ 5. Barreto lives in
    a. California.
    b. Illinois.
    c. Missouri.
    d. Mexico.

_____ 6. Hector Barreto believes Hispanic Americans should
    a. join together.
    b. return to Mexico.
    c. work less.
    d. leave the USHCC.

The Arts and Technology

▲ This is one of Bernardo Fort-Brescia's high-rise buildings in Miami, Florida.

Modern Architecture. In 1977, a group of young architects founded Arquitectonica in Miami. The name means "architectural" in Spanish. The business's projects have included private homes and tall apartment buildings. They have also built office towers, shopping centers, and resorts. Over 50 architects, designers, and planners have developed these projects. Arquitectonica now has its business offices not only in Miami, but also New York, Chicago, and San Francisco. Bernardo Fort-Brescia, born in Peru, and his wife, Laurinda Spear, are the founders and heads of the corporation. They have received many design awards for their projects.

1. What makes this high-rise building different from most such buildings you have seen?

    _____

    _____

2. What other businesses can you name that have Spanish names? _____

    _____

CHAPTER REVIEW: CRITICAL THINKING

1. Why do Hispanic-owned businesses do well in states where the most Hispanic Americans live? _____

    _____

2. How do you explain the move from farm work to blue- and white-collar jobs in the Hispanic-American population? _____

    _____

Chapter 16 HISPANIC AMERICANS IN POLITICS

AIM: What elective offices do Hispanic Americans hold? Why have more Hispanic Americans been elected to office in the past twenty years?

1. Over the past 30 years Hispanic Americans have gained a greater voice in political affairs. In 1988, there were over 3,200 Hispanic Americans holding elective office. Voters have elected Hispanic Americans at nearly every level of government.

2. Why have more and more Hispanic Americans been elected to national, state, and local office? One reason is increased political organization. During the 1960s, Hispanic Americans joined political groups such as MAPA (the Mexican American Political Association) to further their goals. The Raza Unida party was founded in 1970. At the same time, Hispanic Americans became more active in the Democratic and Republican parties.

3. Greater voter participation is another reason for the election of more Hispanic Americans. After World War II, many Mexican Americans, Puerto Ricans, and new Hispanic immigrants moved to the cities. As the growing Hispanic American population concentrated in the cities, their political power grew as well. Hispanic Americans organized themselves to urge people to register to vote and to actually vote. In the past, fewer Hispanic Americans voted than did most other American groups. This is now changing.

4. During the 1960s, voters began electing Hispanic Americans to Congress. For example, Texans elected Henry B. González and Eligio de la Garza. New Yorkers elected Herman Badillo, and New Mexicans elected Manuel Luján, Jr. By 1987, there were 10 Hispanic Americans in Congress, all in the House of Representatives. Nine were Mexican Americans, including Estebán Torres from California, and one was Puerto Rican.

5. More Hispanic Americans are also being elected to political office at the state level. Recent state governors include Jerry Apodaca (1975–79) and Toney Anaya (1983–87) of New Mexico and Raúl H. Castro of Arizona (1975–77). In 1986, Bob Martínez became Florida's first Hispanic-American governor. As of 1987, there were 117 Hispanic Americans serving in 19 state legislatures.

6. Voters have elected several thousand Hispanic Americans to office at the local level. Hispanic-American mayors elected in the 1980s include Federico Peña of Denver, Henry Cisneros of San Antonio, and Xavier Suárez of Miami. Fernando Ferrer was elected borough president of the Bronx, a part of New York City. In 1988, there were four Hispanic Americans serving as Chicago aldermen. Many Hispanic-American city council members and school board officials have been elected.

7. In the past 25 years, women have increased their role in politics. By the mid-1980s, Irma Rangel, Lena Guerrero, and Judy Zaffirini were in the Texas state legislature. Gloria Molina was the first female Hispanic American elected to the California State Assembly in 1982 and the Los Angeles City Council in 1987.

▲ Some of the members of the Congressional Hispanic Caucus, in Washington, D.C.

Understanding What You Have Read

A. For each position listed below, write the name of one Hispanic American who once held or now holds that elected position. Use the information in this chapter or facts about a recent election.

1. Member of the U.S. House of Representatives: _____ from the state of

_____.

2. State-level lawmaker: _____ in the state of _____.

3. Mayor: _____ of the city of _____.

4. Elected city or town official (but not mayor) _____ in the city or town of

_____.

B. Write the main idea of the following paragraphs.

1. *Paragraph 2:* _____

2. *Paragraph 6:* _____

Building Geography Skills

Study the graph. Then answer the questions.

1. Which group had the smallest percentage of its members voting in each election?

_____

2. Did a larger, a smaller, or the same percentage of Hispanic Americans vote in the 1984 election as compared to the 1980 election?

_____

3. Use the information in this chapter and in this graph to predict what will happen to the percentage of Hispanic Americans who will vote over the next 10 years. Explain why you made the prediction you did.

_____

_____

_____

_____

Who Voted in the U.S. National Elections?

Percentage of the Group Who Voted

Hispanics*   Blacks   Whites

*Hispanics of any race or ethnic background

Source: U.S. Bureau of the Census

Esteban Edward Torres. When Esteban Edward Torres ran for Congress in California in 1982 his campaign slogan was "Autoworker to Ambassador, the American Dream." If this was the American dream, then Torres had worked hard to make it a reality.

Torres was born in Miami, Arizona. He served in the army during the Korean War. After leaving the army in 1953, he worked as an assembly-line worker at an auto plant in Los Angeles. He became active in the United Auto Workers Union (UAW). In 1968 he founded the East Los Angeles Community Union (TELACU). This organization grew to become one of the largest antipoverty agencies in the nation.

The attention Torres got from TELACU led to his being appointed ambassador to the United Nations Educational, Scientific and Cultural Organization (UNESCO) in 1977. Then he was made a Hispanic affairs adviser to President Jimmy Carter in 1979. After he became a congressman, Torres became a strong critic of hazardous-waste disposal. In his third term in Congress, Torres became a leader and spokesman for other Hispanic-American congressmen. He was recently elected chairman of the Congressional Hispanic Caucus and fights for the rights of Hispanic Americans everywhere.

Recalling the Facts

Choose each correct answer and write the letter in the space provided.

_____ 1. Before entering public service, Esteban Torres was
   a. a race-car driver.
   b. a construction worker.
   c. an auto worker.

_____ 2. The organization Torres founded was
   a. UNESCO.
   b. TELACU.
   c. UAW.

_____ 3. Torres was an adviser to President
   a. Carter.
   b. Reagan.
   c. Ford.

_____ 4. Congressman Torres was first elected to Congress in
   a. 1980.
   b. 1982.
   c. 1984.

_____ 5. Today Torres is chairman of
   a. the Congressional Hispanic Caucus.
   b. UNESCO.
   c. the Senate.

_____ 6. One issue Torres feels strongly about is
   a. mass transit.
   b. tighter immigration laws.
   c. hazardous-waste disposal.

Using Primary Sources

Joseph Montoya was elected to the U.S. Senate in 1965 and served New Mexico there until 1977, a year before his death. Senator Montoya worked hard for the rights of Hispanic Americans and all the people of his home state. The following excerpt is from a speech he delivered in July 1974. It tells about the real meaning of the American Revolution for young Americans today.

It is not enough that the rights of man should be written in the books of philosophers and in the hearts of good people. It is not even enough that they should be written into our Constitution or declared in the speeches of the Fourth of July. Instead, it is necessary that those who claim these rights also claim the responsibility for preserving them, with God's help.

1. Why do you think that Senator Montoya aimed his speech particularly to young people? _____

_____

2. How can you help preserve your rights as an American? _____

_____

CHAPTER REVIEW: CRITICAL THINKING

1. What are some of the reasons for the increased number of Hispanic Americans elected to office? _____

_____

2. What are some of the ways that elected Hispanic Americans can help make life in the United States better for all Americans? _____

_____

Chapter 17 FEDERAL APPOINTEES

AIM: What Hispanic-American appointees have recently served in the United States? What positions have they held?

1. Unlike elected officials, *appointees* are chosen for their government positions by the president or other high-ranking officials. The growing number of Hispanic-American federal appointments shows Hispanic America's growing political strength.

2. Beginning with the 1960s, more Hispanic Americans were appointed to federal government positions. Presidents Lyndon Johnson and Richard Nixon were both from the Southwest. They knew the importance of Hispanic-American votes and the need of Hispanic Americans to be recognized for their accomplishments. These two presidents appointed several Hispanic Americans to federal positions. President Johnson appointed Vicente T. Ximenes chairman of the President's Cabinet Committee on Mexican-American Affairs. Johnson made Hector P. García a member of the U.S. delegation to the UN. Johnson also appointed Superior Court Judge Raúl H. Castro as U.S. ambassador to El Salvador in 1965. Ten years later, Castro became the first Hispanic-American governor of Arizona.

3. President Nixon appointed Ramona A. Bañuelos as the first Hispanic-American treasurer of the United States in 1971. Nixon also made Phillip V. Sánchez ambassador to Honduras in 1973. Later, Sánchez became ambassador to Colombia. Fernando E. C. de Baca, who was western regional director of the Department of Health, Education, and Welfare, was named President Nixon's special assistant for Hispanic affairs. President Jimmy Carter also appointed a number of Hispanic Americans to important positions. Dr. Julián Nava was the first Mexican American to be appointed ambassador to Mexico.

4. During the eight years of the Reagan administration, a growing number of Hispanic-American women were appointed to high places. In 1983, Katherine Dávalos Ortega became the second Hispanic-American woman to be appointed treasurer of the United States. Patricia Díaz Dennis, a Mexican-American lawyer, was appointed a member of the National Labor Relations Board. Linda Chávez was appointed staff director of the United States Commission on Civil Rights in 1983. Two years later, she was made deputy assistant to the president and director of the Office of Public Liaison.

5. Hispanic-American federal appointees continue to help Hispanic Americans and other citizens find jobs, housing, and social services. They serve their president and country both at home and in distant lands.

▲ Dr. Héctor García, founder of the American G.I. Forum, with President Ronald Reagan at a meeting of that group.

Understanding What You Have Read

Match each person in Column A with the correct description in Column B. Write the correct letter in each blank.

Column A	Column B
_____ 1. Ronald Reagan	a. first Mexican American appointed ambassador to Mexico
_____ 2. Julian Nava	b. chairman of the president's Cabinet Committee on Mexican-American Affairs during the Johnson administration
_____ 3. Lyndon Johnson	c. first Hispanic American governor of Arizona who has served as a U.S. ambassador
_____ 4. Raúl H. Castro	d. president who appointed Dr. Hector García to the U.S. delegation to the United Nations
_____ 5. Ramona A. Bañuelos	e. president who appointed Patricia Díaz Dennis to the National Labor Relations Board
_____ 6. Vicente T. Ximenes	f. first Hispanic-American treasurer of the United States.

Daily Life

Volunteers. VISTA is one of nine volunteer programs sponsored by ACTION, the federal volunteer agency in Washington. About 15 percent of VISTA volunteers, according to ACTION's director, Donna Alvarado, are Hispanic Americans. Recently, one of these was 38-year-old Doris Navarro.

Navarro was a volunteer at the Latino Youth High School in southwest Chicago. The small school is specially designed to help Hispanic-American youths who have previously dropped out of high school. Part of her job, Navarro has said, is "showing them that they can make something of their lives." As the school intake counselor, she enrolled students, helped them choose their courses, and tracked their progress in school and after graduation. Volunteering, says Navarro, "makes you feel good about yourself and it helps in areas that wouldn't get help in the first place."

▲ Members of Volunteers in Service to America (VISTA) fight poverty in urban and rural communities in the United States.

1. Why do you think Doris Navarro kept track of her students' progress after they graduated? _____

_____

2. Do you think volunteer groups like VISTA are valuable? Why or why not?

_____

_____

Spotlight on People

Katherine Dávalos Ortega. Take a look at a recent dollar bill. Just to the left of the picture of George Washington you will see the title "Treasurer of the United States." Above that title is the signature of Katherine Dávalos Ortega.

Katherine Dávalos Ortega was born in 1934, one of nine children. She earned a degree with honors from a New Mexico college. Ortega went to work as a tax supervisor at a large accounting firm. In 1972, she got a job as a cashier at a bank. Within three years, she had worked her way up to the post of vice-president of the bank.

In 1983, President Ronald Reagan appointed Ortega to be the treasurer of the United States. President Reagan said to Treasurer Ortega: "You prove that the American dream is alive and well. I can't think of a better name to have on our money than Katherine Ortega."

In 1984, the Republican party met to choose Reagan to run again for president later that year. The Republicans selected Ortega to give the **keynote address** at their convention. The keynote address is one of the most important speeches given at a political convention. In her speech, Ortega said the following: "We see America not as a nation divided by region or race or creed or sex or ethnic group. We take pride in our individual heritage; that which makes us unique [special]. But the pride we pass on to future generations is the proud heritage of being Americans."

Recalling the Facts

1. Before Ortega was appointed to be the treasurer of the United States, what jobs did she hold? _____

   _____

2. Which president appointed Ortega to her federal post as treasurer? _____

   _____

3. What does the term *keynote address* mean? _____

   _____

4. What two things did Ortega say she took pride in? _____

   _____

Using Primary Sources

Dr. Héctor García, founder of the American G.I. Forum, has served under more U.S. presidents than any other living Hispanic American. In 1984, he received the Medal of Freedom, the highest honor a president can give a civilian, from President Ronald Reagan. Soon after, Dr. García talked about three of the presidents he has served under.

[About John F. Kennedy]: In 1961, I was the first Hispanic that Kennedy appointed to any position. Barely a month after he took office, . . . I got a diplomatic passport that said "Hector García, Representative of the President of the United States." It was a great honor. . . . I had it told to me time and time again by John F. Kennedy, "Dr. García, we have the Hispanic people in Texas to thank for electing me president."

[About Lyndon B. Johnson]: We established a close relationship based on friendship and trust. He talked to me many, many times and I happen to have had the pleasure of knowing him as senator, vice-president and president. . . . He appointed me to the United States Commission on Civil Rights. First Hispanic. And he made me ambassador to the United Nations. . . . He opened the door, . . . really, for Mexican Americans and Hispanics in the United States. . . .

[About Jimmy Carter]: I got to know him even before he was president and rode with him in November before the election. Afterwards, he appointed me to a commission [a committee or group] to select judges for the Fifth Circuit Court of Appeals.

1. What were the three positions to which Dr. García had been appointed? _____

    _____

2. To which president do you think Dr. García felt closest? Explain the reasons for your

    opinion. _____

    _____

CHAPTER REVIEW: CRITICAL THINKING

1. If you joined ACTION as a volunteer, what talents or skills could you bring to the job of

    helping people? _____

    _____

2. Why do you think presidents over the past 25 years have appointed more Hispanic Americans to federal positions? _____

    _____

Chapter 18 THE ARTS AND SPORTS

AIM: What contributions are Hispanic Americans making today in the arts and sports?

1. The spirit of the Hispanic culture has added richly to the arts in the United States. The works of Hispanic American painters and sculptors have an important place in museums in New York, Los Angeles, and other major cities. People visiting the Southwest enjoy Mexican-Americans' folk art and crafts. Jewelry, ponchos, blankets, and pottery are among the popular items tourists buy. Miami is a major center for Cuban-American art. The city's bold architecture also reflects the Cuban influence. In Puerto Rico, tourists see that island's own beautiful architecture. They also visit the famous Ponce Art Museum. It has famous works of art from European and Puerto Rican artists.

2. Hispanic Americans have added variety to the kinds of classical and popular dances that Americans enjoy. In fact many classical ballet dance steps were developed in Spain. There are ethnic groups such as Ballet Hispánico of New York and modern dance companies like José Limón Dance Company. Lourdes López and María Teresa de Real are just two examples of Hispanic-American dancers who are well known. López is with the New York City Ballet. Real, who won a silver medal in the Moscow Ballet Competition, is with the Pittsburgh Ballet. Two of America's most popular dances are the **tango** and the **rumba.** The tango came to the United States from South America. The rumba came to the United States from Cuba.

3. Hispanic-American theater began in local communities and expanded to the national level. In the 1960s, social theater groups such as Luis Valdez's El Teatro Campesino did original plays in open fields and town squares. Today, publicly funded groups such as the nationally touring Spanish Repertory Theater perform plays in both Spanish and English.

4. Hispanic Americans have made significant contributions to movies and television. In 1985, *El Norte* became the biggest money-making Hispanic film ever shown in the United States. *El Norte* tells about the difficult flight of two young Guatemalans north to the United States. In 1988, the movies *La Bamba*, *The Milagro Beanfield War*, and *Stand and Deliver* tell about Hispanic Americans. Edward James Olmos stars as a Hispanic-American mathematics teacher in *Stand and Deliver*. Emilio Estevez, Loni Hall, and Linda Carter are among other actors today who have Hispanic heritage.

5. Hispanic Americans are also known in the world of sports. They have long excelled in baseball, boxing, and soccer. Ángel Cordero is one of the world's most famous jockeys. At the 1984 Summer Olympics in Los Angeles, Hispanic Americans won 11 medals for the United States, including five gold medals. Among the Olympic champions was swimmer Pablo Morales in the 400-meter medley relay.

▲ Jockey Ángel Cordero is shown here in the winner's circle after he and Gate Dancer set a new record.

Understanding What You Have Read

A. Place the name of each person below next to the statement that each might have made.

> Lourdes López   Loni Hall   María Teresa de Real
> Angel Cordero   Luis Valdez

_____ 1. I won a silver medal in the Moscow Ballet Competition.

_____ 2. I own a theater company.

_____ 3. I am a famous jockey.

_____ 4. I am an actor.

_____ 5. I am a leading dancer with the New York City Ballet.

B. Write the word or words that correctly complete each sentence.

1. Collections of art from Europe and Puerto Rico are shown in the _____.

2. Ballroom dances from Cuba and South America that became popular in the United States are the _____.

3. A number of Hispanic-American theater groups now perform plays in both Spanish and _____.

4. Hispanic-American athletes won _____ medals at the 1984 Summer Olympics.

5. _____ is a movie about the flight of Guatemalans to the United States.

Daily Life

Read the following information and look at the photograph. Then answer the questions that follow.

Before the last 10 to 15 years, women did not have as many opportunities in sports as men did. Even today the opportunities are not equal. However women have become a lot more active in many sports. These young Hispanic-American women are serious and enthusiastic about competing in the game of basketball.

1. What clues are there in the picture that the game is basketball? _____

_____

2. What do you think is happening at this point in the game? _____

_____

_____

Spotlight on People

Nancy Lopez. A little-known woman golfer amazed the sports world in 1978. Nancy Lopez, a 21-year-old Mexican American, won five professional tournaments in a row.

No other woman golfer had ever had such a string of victories.

However, Lopez had prepared herself for victory for many years. She began playing golf at age eight. Lopez's mother had taken up the game for her health and Nancy became interested in it. Lopez's father gave her an old club. She soon was playing better than her parents.

Lopez's parents encouraged her talent. They paid for her equipment and lessons. At age 12, Nancy was the women's champion of New Mexico, her home state.

Mental toughness is an important part of golf. Lopez has remained strong through tragedy and heartbreak. Her mother died the year Lopez turned professional. Lopez's first marriage ended and as a Roman Catholic, she was upset.

However, Lopez continued playing golf. At the height of her career, she married again. Lopez cut back her golf when her daughter, Ashley, was born. "Ashley is definitely more important than golf," she said.

Lopez made a comeback in 1985. In that year, she won five tournaments and was Woman Athlete of the Year. Today, she has recaptured her place among the very best women golfers.

Recalling the Facts

Choose each correct answer and write the letter in the space provided.

_____ 1. Nancy Lopez is a successful
  a. baseball player.
  b. golfer.
  c. tennis player.

_____ 2. Early in her professional career, Lopez won
  a. three tournaments in a row.
  b. four tournaments in a row.
  c. five tournaments in a row.

_____ 3. Lopez started playing golf when she was
  a. eight.
  b. twelve.
  c. twenty-one.

_____ 4. The year Lopez turned professional,
  a. her father died.
  b. she had a baby.
  c. her mother died.

_____ 5. When Lopez remarried and had a child, she
  a. cut back on her golf.
  b. gave up golf completely.
  c. was unhappy.

_____ 6. In 1985, Lopez
  a. retired.
  b. married.
  c. made a comeback.

The Arts and Technology:

Popular Music. Vikki Carr is a popular singer who also cares about Hispanic-American concerns. Carr was born in El Paso, Texas, and grew up in San Gabriel Valley near Los Angeles. When she was a teenager she sang on weekends with local bands. After graduating from high school, Carr joined Pepe Callahan's Mexican-Irish Band.

In the 1960s, Carr began recording songs. Her big break came in 1967 when her hit "It Must Be Him" reached the top three on the pop charts. She had five other hit singles in the late 1960s and early 1970s. Today, Carr's albums continue to be best-sellers.

▲ Vicki Carr sang at the Republican National Convention.

1. Why, do you think, do most singers start their careers singing locally? _____

    _____

2. What gave Vikki Carr her big break? _____

    _____

CHAPTER REVIEW: CRITICAL THINKING ▰▰▰

There are many famous Hispanic Americans in the United States. **Hispanic Americans** have made great contributions in the arts and sports.

1. Some people say that the arts and sports bring people of all **cultural backgrounds** together.

    Why might this be so? _____

    _____

2. Select one of these famous Hispanic Americans: Richard Vasquez, Jim Plunkett, Lee Trevino, Joan Baez, Pancho Gonzales, Fernando Valenzuela, Vanna White, and Celia Cruz. Write a newspaper article on your selected person and display it for other members of your class to read.

Chapter 19 SCIENCE AND TECHNOLOGY

AIM: What contributions have Hispanic Americans made in the sciences and technology?

1. Many Hispanic Americans are finding exciting opportunities in the sciences and technology. The sciences and technology will be major industries of the twenty-first century.

2. Two Hispanic Americans are astronauts at the Kennedy Space Center in Florida. Rodolfo Nier Vela is a university teacher, author, and expert on telecommunications. Telecommunication is communication over a distance by means of radio, telephone, or telegraph. Vela was a member of the 1985 United States space shuttle program. His role was to put into orbit the *Morelos II* for Mexico. The *Morelos II* is Mexico's second telecommunications satellite. In 1986, Franklin Chang-Díaz spoke to television viewers in Spanish from the space shuttle *Columbia*. He became the first Hispanic American in space.

3. Hispanic Americans are among the Nobel Prize winners in science. The Nobel Prize is awarded to outstanding scientists and writers and to leaders whose work helps promote peace. Severo Ochoa won the Nobel Prize in physiology in 1959. Physiology is the study of chemical and physical qualities of living matter. Ochoa had discovered a way to make RNA in a test tube. RNA is an acid in cells that controls cell activity. In 1968, Luis W. Alvarez won the Nobel Prize in physics. Physics is the science of matter and energy. Alvarez discovered many subatomic particles.

4. A number of Hispanic Americans have created new products and services for technology. Electrical engineer Rosario Carrillo and three fellow scientists founded Alamo Technology, Inc., in 1981. This multi-million-dollar company designs system integration and engine testing for the air force. Peter O'Compo began the O'Compo Corporation in California. This company makes pre-engineered steel buildings. By pre-engineering a building, steel sections can be planned and formed to the right size ahead of time.

5. Hispanic-American women are among the women in the United States who are today making important contributions to the fields of science and technology. Women have become more active in the sciences and technology in the last 10 or 15 years. Before that, women were often discouraged from taking advanced courses in those fields. Rita Marinita Maldonado-Bear received her doctorate degree from New York University in 1969. She has been a professor of finance and economics. She has also been an adviser to large banks. Elena Raquel Martínez was born in Cuba. She studied at the University of Madrid in Spain and at the University of Havana in Cuba. Today she lives in Miami, Florida, where she specializes in orthopedic, or bone, surgery. Science and technology can greatly improve the lives of Americans.

▲ Young women such as these are encouraged to take courses in science and technology.

Understanding What You Have Read

Match each person or thing in column A with the correct description in column B. Write the correct letter in each blank.

Column A

_____ 1. *Morelos II*

_____ 2. Luis Alvarez

_____ 3. Franklin Chang-Díaz

_____ 4. Severo Ochoa

_____ 5. O'Compo Corporation

_____ 6. Rita Maldonado-Bear

_____ 7. Elena Raquel Martínez

_____ 8. telecommunications

Column B

a. a bone surgeon

b. makes pre-engineered steel buildings

c. radio and telephone

d. won Nobel Prize in physics

e. a telecommunications satellite

f. discovered a way to make RNA

g. advisor to large banks

h. the first Hispanic American in space

Daily Life

In the Classroom. Before Jaime Escalante came to Garfield High School in East Los Angeles, the students were not doing well. Effective teaching was not going on in this mostly Hispanic American school. Escalante, a mathematics teacher, changed things at the school.

Escalante is a Bolivian immigrant. He spoke no English until he was 33 years old. When he became a teacher, he wanted his students to like learning. Some of his ways of getting students interested include throwing a red pillow at them, urging them to shout out answers, and making mistakes to see if his students will catch him. His methods worked. His students learned and enjoyed it!

A movie called *Stand and Deliver* has been made about Escalante. Escalante is played by Edward James Olmos. Of the 18 Hispanic-American students portrayed in the movie, some have graduated from college and others are in graduate school.

1. How do you think Jaime Escalante is able to get his students excited about studying math?_____

_____

_____

_____

2. If you were a teacher, how would you try to make school more interesting for your students? _____

_____

_____

_____

Spotlight on People

Franklin Chang-Díaz. In January 1986, Hispanic television viewers in the United States and Latin America witnessed an exciting event. They watched as an American astronaut spoke to them in Spanish from the space shuttle *Columbia*.

The astronaut was Franklin Chang-Díaz. He was the first Hispanic American in space. Chang-Díaz was well qualified to talk about what life in space is like. He is a scientist as well as an astronaut.

Chang-Díaz was born and raised in Costa Rica. His grandfather had come to Costa Rica from China. As a child, Franklin Chang-Díaz imagined he was an astronaut while playing in his backyard. In 1969, he came to the United States to turn his childhood dream into a reality. He studied mechanical engineering at the University of Connecticut. In 1977, he earned a doctorate degree in physics from Massachusetts Institute of Technology. Three years later, he was one of 19 people selected for the **NASA** space program.

He was part of the ground system crew during the first space lab mission in 1983. After a number of delays, he went into space in 1986. He hopes that his unique videotape of life aboard the *Columbia* will help bring Latin America and the United States closer together in the search for scientific knowledge. As a scientist, he is working on a rocket that will increase the speed of a spacecraft up to 3,000,000 miles per hour.

Recalling the Facts

Choose each correct answer and write the letter in the space provided.

_____ 1. Franklin Chang-Díaz is originally from
  a. Costa Rica.
  b. China.
  c. Colombia.

_____ 2. Besides being an astronaut, Chang-Díaz is a
  a. writer.
  b. filmmaker.
  c. scientist.

_____ 3. Chang-Díaz took his first flight into space in
  a. 1983. b. 1986. c. 1988.

_____ 4. During his space flight, Chang-Díaz
  a. mostly slept.
  b. wrote a scientific article in Spanish.
  c. made a video for television in Spanish.

_____ 5. Chang-Díaz earned his doctorate degree from the
  a. California Institute of Technology.
  b. Massachusetts Institute of Technology.
  c. University of Connecticut.

_____ 6. Chang-Díaz is working on a new kind of
  a. high-speed rocket.
  b. computer for outer space.
  c. space suit for astronauts.

The Arts and Technology:

Science and Reseach. In 1959, Severo Ochoa won the Nobel Prize in physiology. He had discovered a way to make RNA (ribonucleic acid) in the test tube. RNA is a substance found in all living cells. It helps to transmit inherited traits by carrying out the instructions of DNA (deoxyribonucleic acid). DNA is a similar substance, found in cells, that carries hereditary instructions. Ochoa discovered an enzyme that controls the formation of RNA. He used the enzyme to produce RNA in his laboratory. Ochoa shared his Nobel Prize with American Arthur Kornberg. Kornberg first developed a way to make DNA in a test tube.

▲ Dr. Severo Ochoa, who was born in Spain, has taught at universities in Spain, Germany, England, and the United States. He became an American citizen in 1956.

1. What object or thing does the RNA molecule resemble? _____
   _____

2. How do you think Ochoa and Kornberg helped one another with their discoveries?
   _____
   _____

CHAPTER REVIEW: CRITICAL THINKING

Today, Hispanic-American men and women can choose work in the sciences and technology.

1. If you could interview Franklin Chang-Díaz about his trip into space, what two questions would you ask him? _____
   _____

2. Why, do you think, are the fields of sciences and technology going to be the major industries of the twenty-first century? _____
   _____

Chapter 20 HISPANIC AMERICANS TODAY

AIM: What does the future hold for Hispanic Americans?

1. There are over 19 million Hispanic Americans in the United States today. They are the second largest minority group, after Black Americans. Nearly 60 percent of all Hispanic Americans are Mexican Americans. The population growth rate for Hispanic Americans is nearly five times that of the country as a whole. A large immigrant population accounts for some of the rapid growth. By 2000, it is predicted that Hispanic Americans will probably be the largest minority in the United States.

2. One-half of all Hispanic Americans live in just two states—California and Texas. If the Hispanic Americans in New York and Florida are added, this accounts for about three-fourths of the nation's Hispanic Americans.

3. More Hispanic Americans work in blue-collar jobs than do Blacks and Anglo Americans—about 45 percent. Nearly 35 percent have white-collar jobs. By 1987, the average Hispanic-American family income was $22,900. However, the average Cuban-American family income was $27,500, well above the national average for other Hispanic-American families.

▲ Cuban Americans applaud after being sworn in as United States citizens.

4. Hispanic Americans are working to overcome discrimination and lack of education. Those Hispanic Americans without a good education do not have the skills to get better jobs. Although many Hispanic Americans have trouble with the English language, one of the main reasons Hispanics drop out of school is that they must work to help out at home. There is a lack of agreement about bilingual education in many parts of the country. With bilingual education, children learn the difficult content of courses in Spanish while learning to speak English.

5. One group of Hispanic people has had an especially serious problem. This group is mostly made up of recent **undocumented immigrants** from Mexico. Undocumented means they are without the necessary papers to be allowed into the United States. Members of this group are paid very low wages and usually live in poor conditions. This group feels, however, that the opportunities in the United States are better than those in Mexico. The United States has been trying to stop them from entering the country illegally.

6. In 1986, Congress passed the **Simpson-Rodino Act.** This new law said that employers who hired undocumented immigrants would be fined, or have to pay the government money as punishment. At the same time, the act offered **amnesty** to about 3 million undocumented immigrants already in the United States. Amnesty is a political pardon. Under the **amnesty program,** immigrants who have been in the United States at least five years can stay and apply for citizenship.

7. The growth rate of Hispanic Americans is not yet matched by their income, education, and political power. As more Hispanic Americans stay in school and go on to college, however, they are able to compete with other Americans for skilled and professional jobs. At the same time they are increasing their political, economic, and social position. Hispanic Americans are proud, energetic, and creative Americans. They are building a great future for themselves and a better America.

Understanding What You Have Read

A. Write the correct word or words from the list that best complete each sentence.

1990	education	Texas	quarter
Colorado	2000	housing	half

1. Nearly half of all Hispanic Americans live in California and _____.

2. By the year _____ , Hispanic Americans may be the largest minority group in the United States.

3. Many_____ Hispanic-American immigrants came from Mexico.

4. The future of Hispanic Americans lies in better _____.

B. In each of the sentences that follow, the underlined word makes the sentence true or false. If the sentence is true, write **T** in the blank before it. If it is false, write the word or words that will make it true.

_____ 1. Cuban-American family income is <u>higher</u> than that of most other Hispanic Americans.

_____ 2. Close to three-fourths of all Hispanics in the United States live in just <u>seven </u>states.

_____ 3. many Hispanic youths drop out of school because of <u>language and financial </u>problems.

_____ 4. The Simpson-Rodino Act will fine <u>workers </u>who do not obey the law.

Linking Past to Present

1. There were about 8,679,000 Mexican Americans in the United States in 1980. Between 1980 and 1987 the population grew by about how many more Mexican Americans?

   _____

2. Which group grew the least between 1980 and 1987?

   _____

3. Which group grew more between 1980 and 1987, Puerto Ricans or "other Hispanics"?

   _____

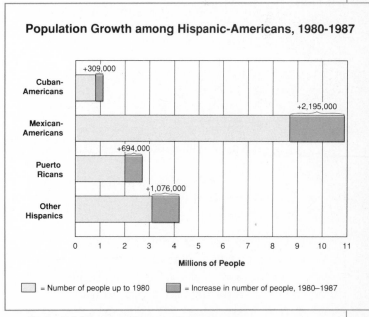

Population Growth among Hispanic-Americans, 1980-1987

Cuban-Americans: +309,000
Mexican-Americans: +2,195,000
Puerto Ricans: +694,000
Other Hispanics: +1,076,000

Millions of People

☐ = Number of people up to 1980   ▨ = Increase in number of people, 1980–1987

Source: U.S. Department of Commerce, Bureau of the Census; Strategy Research Corporation.

Spotlight on People

Kira Alvarez. Kira Alvarez has a dream. It is to one day become the first United States ambassador to Cuba. With the United States and the Soviet Union getting along better, the renewal of relations between Cuba and the United States might occur.

Whether this happens or not, Alvarez's future promises to be a bright one. This young Cuban American is a junior at Harvard University. She is studying government. Alvarez's parents left Castro's Cuba in 1965. They settled in Miami. Her father is a graduate of the University of Havana. When he came to the United States, he worked as a dishwasher to feed his family. He saved his money and soon started his own bakery in Miami. He encouraged his children to study hard and make something of themselves. Today, Alvarez's two brothers are engineers. One sister is a speech teacher and the other a lawyer. As the youngest child, Alvarez says she worked extremely hard "to show them I was just as good as they were."

She graduated first in a class of 500 students at Miami High School. She was class valedictorian. At Harvard, Alvarez is production manager of *The Harvard International Review*. She is also a member of the International Relations Council. "The council has a model United Nations program," she says. "We put on two conferences each year in which high school and college students role play at being UN delegates."

Recalling the Facts

Choose each correct answer and write the letter in the space provided.

_____ 1. Kira Alvarez's parents came to the United States in
  a. 1960. b. 1965. c. 1968.

_____ 2. In Miami, Alvarez's family runs a
  a. restaurant.
  b. grocery store.
  c. bakery.

_____ 3. Alvarez was motivated to do well by
  a. a grade school teacher.
  b. her best friend.
  c. her family.

_____ 4. The International Relations Council at Harvard runs
  a. a workshop for poor students.
  b. a model UN program for students.
  c. an international festival.

_____ 5. At Harvard, Alvarez is majoring in
  a. government.
  b. English.
  c. science.

_____ 6. One day, Alvarez would like to be the
  a. first woman vice president of the United States.
  b. U.S. ambassador to Cuba.
  c. first Hispanic-American college president.

Using Primary Sources

A Speech. Dr. Joseph A. Fernandez became Superintendent of schools for the Dade County Public Schools in Miami, Florida, in 1987. Over one-quarter of a million students and 150,000 adults attended these schools. It is the fourth largest school system in the United States. Dr. Fernandez was born in New York City of Puerto Rican parents. Here is part of the speech he gave to school officials at the opening of the schools at the end of the summer in 1987.

> Our task will be to continue to encourage academic excellence.... We need to raise our level of expectancy of *all* students and thus reduce the achievement gap between minority and non-minority students. We must increase the ability of minority students to speak and write standard English. We must turn out students who are bilingual [able to speak two languages] and biliterate [able to read two languages]. We must improve students' abilities to think critically. We must see that vocational [training in a skill or trade] programs will prepare students for high-technology jobs.
>
> We need to have more students like Esteban Torres. *Newsweek* magazine named the 18-year-old valedictorian [the student with the highest rank in a graduating class who gives a speech at graduation] of Coral Gables Senior High School one of America's Heroes this past July Fourth (1987). Esteban is a former Mariel refugee (from Cuba) who came to Miami in 1980, unable to speak English. He will join the freshman class at Massachussets Institute of Technology (MIT) this fall as an engineering major.

1. What are three of the goals that Dr. Fernandez mentioned in his speech?_____

   _____

   _____

2. Dr. Fernandez wants to improve students' abilities to think critically. List three critical thinking skills you have been asked to use in the Chapter Review: Critical Thinking

   sections of this book._____

   _____

   _____

CHAPTER REVIEW: CRITICAL THINKING

When you **predict,** you look ahead and make a guess about what may happen next. A good prediction needs to be based on facts.

1. What do you predict will be the results of the 1986 amnesty law over the next 10 years? Do

   you think the amnesty law was a good one? Why or why not? _____

   _____

2. How do you think becoming the largest minority group in the United States will affect

   Hispanic Americans? Be specific. Support your prediction. _____

   _____

UNIT 4 REVIEW

Summary of the Unit

A few of the most important events and facts presented in Unit 4 are listed below. Write these in your notebook and add four more.

1. Thousands of businesses are owned by Hispanic Americans today, ranging from small grocery stores to major corporations.
2. Hispanic Americans serve as elected officials at nearly every level of government from small town mayor to U.S. representative in Congress.
3. Hispanic Americans have been appointed in the federal government to high posts in the treasury and in labor, civil rights, and volunteer organizations. A number of Hispanic Americans are United States ambassadors to foreign countries.
4. Hispanic Americans are making major contributions in the fine arts, theater, music, television, movies, and sports.
5. Two Hispanic Americans have been awarded Nobel prizes in science. A number of them have contributed to the United States space program, including astronaut-scientist Franklin Chang-Díaz.
6. Hispanic Americans are overcoming prejudice, poverty, and injustice and are succeeding in many areas of American life.

Understanding What You Have Read

Choose each correct answer and write the letter in the space provided.

_____ 1. Today Hispanic-American executives can be found in
    a. only Hispanic-owned businesses.
    b. only businesses outside the United States.
    c. many non-Hispanic businesses.

_____ 2. States with recent or present Hispanic-American governors include
    a. Florida, New Mexico, and Arizona.
    b. California, New Jersey, and Colorado.
    c. New York, Florida, and Nevada.

_____ 3. Beginning in the 1960s, United States presidents have appointed to high federal positions
    a. fewer Hispanic Americans than in the 1940s and 1950s.
    b. more Hispanic Americans than in the 1940s and 1950s.
    c. about the same number of Hispanic Americans as in the 1940s and 1950s.

_____ 4. The highest-grossing Hispanic film released in the United States is
    a. *The Milagro Beanfield War.*
    b. *Crossover Dreams.*
    c. *El Norte.*

_____ 5. Hispanic Americans have made a great contribution to the
    a. computer sciences.
    b. U.S. space program.
    c. development of new food sources.

_____ **6.** About a quarter of all Hispanic Americans are
  a. poor.
  b. rich.
  c. middle class.

Developing Ideas and Skills—Using Time Lines

Study the time line. Then answer the questions .

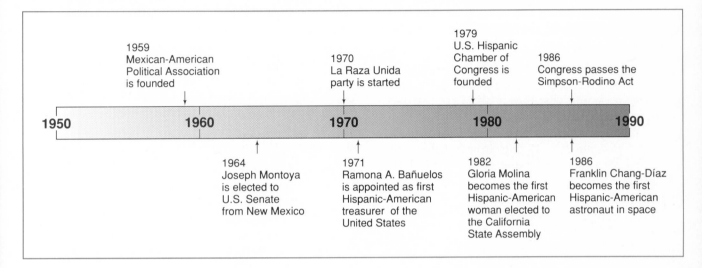

1. Which organization was founded first, the Mexican American Political Association or the

   La Raza Unida party?_____

2. In what year was the Simpson-Rodino Act passed by Congress?_____

3. Which happened first, the first Hispanic-American woman was elected to the California
   State Assembly or the first Hispanic American was appointed to be treasurer of the United

   States?_____

4. Who was the first Hispanic-American astronaut in space and in what year did his space

   flight occur?_____

Making History Live

1. Write a short essay about a famous Hispanic-American actor, musician, or athlete whom
   you admire. List three events or influences in that person's life that helped him or her
   succeed. Research your report in the library.
2. Join with other students to make a classroom bulletin-board display devoted to Hispanic
   Americans today. Include magazine pictures and photographs as well as original student
   artwork in the display. Show the wide range of Hispanic-American contributions to our
   society, including Hispanic-American products, celebrities, culture, and so forth.

Glossary

adobe sun-dried bricks of earth and straw (p. 23)

aliens foreigners living in one country while citizens of another country (p. 20)

amnesty a political pardon of a large group of people (p. 84)

amnesty program a government program begun in 1986. It allows foreigners who have lived in the United States illegally for at least five years to become legal residents and apply for United States citizenship. (p. 84)

Aztecs Native Americans who ruled Mexico in the early 1500s (p. 40)

barrio a Spanish-speaking neighborhood in a city or town in the United States (p. 2)

Basques a people who live in the Pyrenees between France and Spain (p. 10)

Bay of Pigs invasion an unsuccessful American-supported effort in 1961 to invade Cuba and overthrow the Communist government of Fidel Castro (p. 43)

blockade to cut off a country or enemy troops from supplies and reinforcements (p. 42)

bodega a neighborhood store selling Hispanic groceries (p. 64)

boycott a refusal to buy a product (p. 38)

bracero a Mexican worker allowed into the United States for temporary farm work (p. 24)

bracero **program** an agreement between the United States and Mexico to allow Mexican farm workers to work in the United States. Ended in 1964. (p. 24)

Californios descendants of Spanish settlers who lived in California before 1848 (p. 2)

Chicanos Mexican Americans (p. 38)

colonias Hispanic neighborhoods in large cities (p. 14)

commonwealth a self-governing political unit with ties to the United States (p. 30)

Congressional Medals of Honor the highest awards for military bravery in the United States (p.24)

constitution a set of rules for governing a city, state, or nation (p. 16)

corrido a Mexican folk ballad about real events (p. 13)

Cuban missile crisis dispute between the United States and the Soviet Union in which the United States in 1962 demanded that Soviet missiles be removed from Cuba (p. 42)

discrimination the separate and unequal treatment of people by race, religion, national origin, or other category (p. 24)

El Barrio a large Puerto Rican neighborhood in New York City (p. 46)

exile the forced absence from one's homeland (p. 43)

Foraker Act of 1900 the United States law allowing Puerto Rico to send a nonvoting representative to the United States Congress (p. 7)

Freedom Airlift the removal by airplane in 1965 of Cubans anxious to leave Communist-run Cuba to join in the United States (p. 42)

galleons Spanish sailing ships used from the 1400s to early 1600s (p. 9)

G.I. Bill of Rights a program that gave job training and educational opportunities to veterans of World War II and the Korean War (p. 28)

Great Depression a period in the 1930s when millions of Americans were unemployed (p. 20)

grievance a complaint (p. 4)

Hispanic American an American whose home language is Spanish or whose ancestors or heritage is from Spain or former Spanish colonies (p. 14)

Hispanos descendants of Spanish settlers who lived in what is now the southwestern United States before 1848 (p. 2)

huapangos Mexican cowboy songs (p. 53)

immigrant a person who leaves another country to settle in the United States (p. 2)

immigration the act of leaving another country to settle in the United States (p. 10)

intelligence officer a military officer who gathers and studies information about a country's enemies or possible enemies (p. 34)

jacal a house in Mexico and the American Southwest with a thatched roof and walls made of upright poles or sticks covered with mud or clay (p. 5)

Jones Act of 1917 the United States law that made Puerto Rico a territory of the United States and Puerto Ricans citizens of the United States (p. 7)

keynote address an important speech given at a political convention (p. 74)

labor union an organization formed by workers to win higher wages or better working conditions (p. 25)

la raza the race (p. 38)

mano upper stone used in grinding corn (p. 5)

Mariel boat people some 125,000 people who came to the United States from Cuba in 1980 (p. 54)

metate lower stone used in grinding corn (p. 5)

Mexican American an American of Mexican descent (p. 2)

Mexican Cession lands won by the United States in the Mexican War. Included today's states of California, Nevada, and Utah and parts of New Mexico, Colorado, Arizona, and Wyoming (p. 3)

migrant worker a worker, usually a farm worker, who travels from one temporary job to another (p. 38)

NASA National Aeronautical and Space Agency. The United States government agency responsible for space exploration (p. 82)

New Deal a United States government program to create jobs in the 1930s (p. 20)

Operation Bootstrap Luis Muñoz Marín's program for the economic development of Puerto Rico in the 1940s and 1950s (p. 30)

Operation Serenidad Luis Muñoz Marín's program to encourage creativity in Puerto Rico in the 1940s and 1950s (p. 30)

plantado a Cuban political prisoner in the 1960s (p. 44)

Platt Amendment an amendment passed by the United States Congress added to Cuba's constitution in 1901 as a condition of American withdrawal. It gave the United States the right to protect Cuba's independence. (p. 6)

prejudice dislike without reason of people of other races, religions, or nationalities (p. 14)

Radio Martí an anti-Castro Spanish-language radio station in Miami sending broadcasts to Cuba (p. 54)

rancheras Mexican cowboy songs (p. 53)

raza a term sometimes used by Mexican Americans to refer to themselves; the race; the people (p. 38)

repatriation the return of immigrants to their homeland (p. 20)

ricos wealthy Hispanic Americans and Anglos who married into their families (p. 2)

Rough Riders nickname for the 1st Volunteer Cavalry in the Spanish-American War of 1898 (p. 6)

rumba a ballroom dance of Cuban origins (p. 76)

Simpson-Rodino Act 1986 United States law that punishes employers who hire workers without the papers necessary to live permanently in the United States (p. 84)

Stegomyia fasciata the mosquito responsible for yellow fever (p. 8)

tango a ballroom dance of South American origins (p. 76)

Treaty of Guadalupe Hidalgo the 1848 treaty signed by Mexico and the United States at the end of the Mexican War. Transferred the northern one-third of Mexico to the United States (p. 3)

undocumented immigrant a foreigner who has entered the United States without the proper legal papers (p. 84)

Viet Cong South Vietnamese Communists in the Vietnam War (p. 32)

yellow fever a tropical disease spread by the *Stegomyia* mosquito (p. 8)

Zimmermann note a secret note sent by Germany to Mexico in 1917. Offered to return to Mexico the lands lost to the United States in 1848 if Mexico would side with Germany against the United States. The offer was rejected. (p. 14)

zoot suit a flashy style of suit worn by some groups in the 1940s (p. 27)

Index